West Indian Migration to Britain

West Indian Migration to Britain

A SOCIAL GEOGRAPHY

CERI PEACH

Published for
the Institute of Race Relations, London
by

OXFORD UNIVERSITY PRESS
LONDON   NEW YORK   TORONTO
1968

Oxford University Press, Ely House, London W. 1

GLASGOW NEW YORK TORONTO MELBOURNE WELLINGTON
CAPE TOWN SALISBURY IBADAN NAIROBI LUSAKA ADDIS ABABA
BOMBAY CALCUTTA MADRAS KARACHI LAHORE DACCA
KUALA LUMPUR HONG KONG TOKYO

Printed in Great Britain by
The Camelot Press Ltd., London and Southampton

CONTENTS

LIST OF TABLES

ACKNOWLEDGEMENTS

I would like to acknowledge my very great debt to my teachers in Oxford. Professor Kenneth Kirkwood, Rhodes Professor of Race Relations, supervised me when I was a D.Phil. student and was generous with his time and illuminating in his insight. Professor E. W. Gilbert, now Emeritus Professor of Geography, was greatly encouraging to the work. Above all, my interest in West Indian migration was nurtured by my former tutor and present colleague, Mr. E. Paget, Fellow of Jesus College. He taught me in particular, to examine the differences between social and economic needs: this work embodies many of his other precepts.

My thanks are also due to the late Hugh Gaitskell. His speech in the Commonwealth Immigrants' Bill debate in which he related demand for labour in Great Britain to West Indian migration and a letter in which he elaborated this view, opened up a whole new field for me.

To my parents and my German grandparents who gave me the money to begin this work, I am more grateful than I can say.

Finally, I must thank Miss Celia Phillips of the Institute of Race Relations for her care and tact in the trying work of editing the manuscript.

Maps 1 and 2 are reproduced by permission of the Council of the Institute of British Geographers from Transactions No. 38, 1966.

INTRODUCTION

The nineteenth and twentieth centuries have been the period of greatest economic change and have seen the greatest movements of population. Industrialization demanded large bodies of workmen; concentrations of workmen demanded food, raw materials and markets far beyond the resources of their own countries. It is difficult to say whether population growth demanded industrialization or industrialization demanded increased population but geographically, the effects were bound together. On one hand there was the concentration of population in urban industrial centres; on the other, the areal diffusion of population over the grasslands of North and South America, Australia and New Zealand. Together these economic and population changes helped to form new nations, free of some of the social rigidity of the old, while in the old countries, they created a more cohesive political body in the urban proletariat. Thus, these two population movements—to the open areas and to the slums and villas of the urban areas—were the same in their economic origins, socially dissimilar in their effects but geographically complementary.

The passage of time has removed the open areas, on the whole, for large-scale population movements. The later stages of the great European migration to the U.S.A., Australia and New Zealand were destined increasingly for the towns. As industrialization increased, the rural populations of these countries were attracted to the towns as well. Urban efficiency in services and marketing stimulated rural production. Emphasis shifted in developed areas from production per acre to production per man. The lessening rural man-power was compensated by increasing capitalization. Urbanization in these regions, has been the product of technical progress.

The plight of underdeveloped countries is that with increasing population, they have to seek to increase productivity per acre while productivity per man decreases. In these countries, particularly in the tropics, urbanization, particularly of the largest towns, has become increasingly evident.[1] In these areas, the movement has a large element of instability. In industrialized countries, the population movement has been a positive one, in response to demand for labour. In underdeveloped countries, it is often a movement from rural under-employment to urban unemployment. Thus, while the initial impulse of the industrial revolution offered both diffusion and concentration of population, at least to Europeans, the areas of diffusion are now exhausted, and concentration alone remains. Towns are the new frontier of the great migrations.

The most striking feature of the emergence of the town as the immigrants' destination has been the reversal of direction of emigration. Though Europe continues as a region of emigration, some of the countries have attracted large-scale immigration. The West German federal employment office issued figures in 1963 which showed there were 804,000 foreign workers in the country. Most of these were from southern Europe but non-Europeans numbered 34,000. Of these 15,500 were Asians and 11,400 Africans (including 4,800 Moroccans), Switzerland, France and Britain have all received large population movements from abroad, and the latter two, substantial numbers of coloured immigrants. Algerian Muslims in France seem to have numbered about 520,000 at the end of 1964: at the end of 1960 they numbered about 345,700 out of a total French population of 45,355,000. The number of this group alone was higher than the combined West Indian, Indian, and Pakistani population of Great Britain at that time. The movement of population to regions of high densities has been in existence for some time, but when it appears that Europe is affected, the movement takes on a novel appearance.

Immigration into the traditional centres of emigration seems unusual in other ways, since the growth of nationalism as well as population has tended to close the doors of many traditional countries of immigration. Where immigration continues, there is a great deal of selection. Australia and New Zealand seem to

[1] D. Linton, 'Millionaire Cities Today and Yesterday', *Geography*, 1958, pp. 253–8.

prefer the British most and northern and western Europeans more than those from south and east Europe. Asiatics are hardly countenanced and Negroes not at all. In general, countries that want immigration seek to produce it in the image of the ruling class. Resistance to groups of migrants in these countries grows with the deepening colour of their skin; one might say on a chromatic scale.[1] Yet in Britain, migration has come from the tropics and in Germany from the Middle East and North Africa as well as the Mediterranean countries. Indeed, while the depression and Nazism of the 1930s led to the expulsion and extermination of many minority groups, the economic expansion of the post-war period led to the introduction of new minorities.

The significant fact in the new industrial expansion of Europe is that it has increased the demand not only for skilled workers but for unskilled labour as well. The growing economic gulf between the developed and the undeveloped nations has allowed and perhaps necessitated a radical extension of the areas that supply this need. The movement of West Indians to Britain is essentially one from tropical rural areas to temperate urban areas. While it may at first have seemed to have been brought about by the poverty of the homeland, it now seems that such conditions are permissive not 'push' factors. It is not that poverty is new in the south, it is that industrial prosperity, on its present scale, is new in northern Europe.

To some extent, the positive attraction of the countries of immigration has been masked by political factors. In Britain the movement of immigrants took place within the framework of the Commonwealth and colonial territories. Algeria, until its independence, was considered an integral, if not contiguous part of France. Thus, its large North African population was considered a natural development. The Common Market allowed a freer movement of labour and opened up the Italian man-power reserve to Germany. Thus, most of these movements have taken place within continuous political units. It is possible, therefore, that they were viewed in some quarters not as a response to economic need, but as a failure of political machinery to keep them out.

[1] E. Paget, Oxford lectures on population, 1959 (unpublished).

This has meant that most attention was focussed on the 'push' factors in the sending countries rather than the dynamic attraction of the industrial centres for which the migrants are destined. In Germany, however, the small group of non-European workers in a country with no colonial ties is a significant indication of the strength of demand for labour, for the country at the end of 1963 had not only the 804,000 foreign workers already mentioned, but over 13,000,000 persons resettled from the east.

Thus, since the Second World War and particularly since the mid-1950s, people in Britain became aware of a growing coloured immigrant population. It was a general awareness of the urban population, for immigrants were no longer connected only with the old dockside settlements, but with the inland towns and industrial centres. The image was no longer that of the seaman but of the bus conductor.

The impression of continuous growth was strong, yet the dimensions of the movement from year to year were not accurately known. The Government's unofficial statistics on immigration differed largely from the official count. The debates in Parliament about controlling the movement had sometimes an unreal ring, when there was no common statistical ground on which to fight. There were, too, nice ironies in the exchange of political clothes. Some of the most powerful speeches on the Labour side emphasized the efficacy of the free market economy, of the need not to interfere with the self-regulating economic system, while on the Conservative side there were pleas of the need to over-ride the undoubted economic advantages that immigration brought on social grounds.

The Preliminary Report of the 1961 census showed that from 1951 to 1961 'net migration, whether outward at the beginning or inward later, has been trivial in relation to natural increase'.[1] It added, however, that since 1959 the gain in number from the excess of immigration over emigration had risen and in 1960-1 was estimated to have exceeded the excess of births over deaths. This had not happened since the inward rush of refugees and

[1] Census of England and Wales, 1961, Preliminary Report, H.M.S.O., 1961, p. 6.

repatriation immediately prior to the Second World War.[1] The 1961 census showed that the West Indian-born population of England and Wales was 171,796; that Indian nationals numbered 46,575, and Pakistanis 19,250. These three groups accounted for just over half of 1 per cent of the population of England and Wales.

There was general agreement that London and Birmingham were the main centres of coloured immigration, but before the publication of the 1961 census, estimates of their number in these and other centres varied by a considerable proportion. In 1960, one estimate put the coloured population of Bristol at between 1,000 and 3,000 and Leeds, Coventry and Glasgow in the same range.[2] An estimate of 40,000 West Indians in the London area, given by the same source, was described by another authority as a rash guess.[3] Thus, at the time that the Commonwealth immigration policy of Britain was decided, the volume, trend, and distribution was not accurately known.

There was general agreement that social difficulties arose out of the tendency of coloured immigrants to cluster together. There was a fear of the growth of overcrowded coloured quarters and of the consequent problems of integration. Yet ignorance of the geographical distribution within urban areas was almost as great as that of the distribution in the country as a whole. Since they represented only a 'trivial' part of the country's population increase and a very small proportion of the population itself, their most disturbing characteristic was not so much their total number as their colour, rate of immigration, and their local concentrations.

It might be argued that, with the exception of concentrations of settlement, these are questions for sociologists, demographers, or economists and not for geographers. Yet each of the other characteristics may affect the distribution pattern and may be

[1] Ibid., p. 6.
[2] Donald Wood, *Coloured Immigrants in Britain*, edited by J. A. G. Griffith, Institute of Race Relations, O.U.P., 1960, p. 15.
[3] Ruth Glass, *Newcomers*, George Allen and Unwin, and Centre for Urban Studies, 1960, p. 32.

treated geographically. It is not the subject of discussion but the discipline of analysis that decides whether a subject is geographical, sociological, or whatever. One is interested in building a body of knowledge, not quarrelling for a carcase. Social geography has a legitimate, if limited part to play in studies of population change. It provides a framework on which other studies can be built: it is basic, not catholic.

The view-point of social geography is that social differences give rise to geographical differences and that geographic differences reflect social differences. Herbertson's classic precept may be extended; 'By comparing the histories of the same race in two regions, or of a succession of races in the same region, it should be possible to arrive at some knowledge of the invariable effect of environment on its inhabitants, and permit some estimation of the non-environmental factors in human development.'[1] By comparing the geographical differences of two races in one region, it should be possible to arrive at some knowledge of the social difference between the two. To give an example: the ghetto is the geographical expression of complete social rejection. As a working hypothesis, therefore, it could be assumed that complete absence of segregation is probable only in an environment of complete social acceptance. Therefore, the degree of segregation of two groups on a scale from the ghetto to complete dispersal is a concrete expression of the social attitudes of the groups concerned to each other. There are a number of fascinating studies showing that geographical separation increases with increasing social friction.[2]

At the same time there should be a consistent geographic correlation of supposed cause with supposed effect. For instance, if density of population were considered the major determinant of emigration from the West Indies and there was little correlation between degrees of density and degrees of emigration, there would be grounds for believing that other factors had influenced

[1] A. J. Herbertson, 'The Major Natural Regions', *Geographical Journal*, March 1905, p. 309.

[2] For example, Emrys Jones, 'The Distribution and Segregation of Roman Catholics in Belfast', *Sociological Review*, Vol. 4, 1956.

migration more strongly. Thus, on one hand social geography can help to define the effects of difference through distributions and, on the other, use distributions to help define the nature of the cause.

In writing this book, it often proved impossible to deal with West Indians in isolation from the other two major coloured immigrant groups. Though there are major linguistic, ethnic, religious, and social differences between them and the Pakistanis and Indians, from the point of view of the host society, they were all in the same economic and social position, occupied largely the same type of locality and their distributions were explicable only when they were considered together.

The first three chapters deal with the background to the movement in the West Indies. The next two with the effects of economic and political conditions in Great Britain on immigration. Chapter 6 considers the distribution of immigrants in Great Britain and Chapter 7 the general and particular distributions in urban areas. Chapter 8 summarizes the main conclusions.

Paradoxically, the reader may find it easiest to begin with the conclusion.

CHAPTER I

BACKGROUND TO EMIGRATION

The emigration of West Indians to Great Britain that took place during the 1950s and early 1960s was the largest net outward movement of population to take place from what was formerly the British Caribbean. In spite of the difficulties of obtaining accurate statistics for any of these movements, it seems that the 171,796 persons born in the West Indies, recorded in the 1961 census of England and Wales, is higher than any of the estimates for previous movements of West Indians to a single destination and by the beginning of 1964, the net movement to Britain exceeded the combined totals for all destinations, of the previous highest net migrations. It is likely that the 1961 census figure is 20 per cent too low[1] and that by the beginning of 1966, West Indian-born persons in Britain numbered about 330,000. In the previous highest outward movement from the West Indies to Panama, the U.S.A., and other countries in or around the Caribbean between 1881 and 1921, the net movement was in the order of 200,000 to 250,000.[2]

Emigration, under the conditions which obtained in the West Indies, is not surprising. The West Indies can be summarized as having a small, poor, scattered population, often living at high densities, in the tropics, producing primary products. The expansion of the sugar industry during the eighteenth and nine-teenth centuries had demanded an increasing labour force. This had been supplied first, by an imported African slave population,

[1] See Appendix 2, p. 108.
[2] Based on figures given by R. R. Kuczynski, *Demographic Survey of the British Colonial Empire*, Vol. III, Royal Institute of International Affairs, O.U.P., 1953, pp. 5–7, and G. W. Roberts, *The Population of Jamaica*, Conservation Foundation, C.U.P., 1957, p. 339. This is probably a generous estimate as the figures of both Roberts and Kuczynski are derived, in part, from arbitrary calculations. See Roberts, p. 339 and Kuczynski, pp. 6–7.

then by a pro-natalist policy towards the existing slaves and finally by importing indentured workers from India. However, with the development of new areas of sugar supply in the tropics and of beet sugar in temperate areas, the West Indian sugar industry suffered a relative decline. The West Indies fell from being prized possessions to being the sad, uneconomic rump of Empire. Jamaica and Trinidad, it is true, became independent in 1962, but they were no longer dependent on sugar: bauxite and petroleum products respectively had assumed important roles. With the break-up of the Federation, the hopes for the neat disposal of the expensive necklace of the Lesser Antilles around the necks of these stronger economies has also foundered.

The population continued expanding despite the decline of the sugar industry which had initiated it so that the West Indian islands became characterized by high population densities, high unemployment and underemployment, low G.D.P.s *per capita* and, with the exception of Jamaica, Trinidad, and to a smaller extent Antigua, by low rates of economic growth. The total West Indian population at the time of the 1960 census was 3,763,000 and the average rate of increase in the inter-censal period 1946–60 had been high, 2·28 per cent per annum. Generalizations cover wide variations, of course, and while the density of population was over 1,300 per square mile on Barbados, on the mainland territories of British Guiana and British Honduras it was ten and eight respectively. In terms of Gross Domestic Product *per capita*, the territories were certainly not among the richest in the world, nor were they among the poorest. However, even those territories, such as Jamaica and Trinidad, which had been diversified away from monoculture, were still largely dependent on the export of primary products.

Nevertheless, the view which sees conditions in the West Indies as the dominant force that drives the migration seems misfounded. It is difficult to evaluate separately the push and pull factors, since they exist mainly in relation to each other, but it is possible to do so. As a result, the push forces seem inadequate either alone or as the dominant factor in explaining this movement.

In her extremely important book, Ruth Glass attributed the movement to Britain to the conditions in the West Indies and to the closing of the doors of other countries to West Indian immigration.[1] Her argument is not an important part of her thesis, but it provides a useful basis for examining the supposed relationship of conditions in the West Indies to emigration.

The main causes of migration in the recent post-war period are fairly evident. First, there is the pressure of population. G. W. Roberts's study of the population of Jamaica, the largest of the West Indian islands, shows clearly that the rate of growth of population, already high before the Second World War, has increased since then. 'Indeed since 1950 the island has consistently shown rates of natural increase in excess of 2 per cent which, despite some emigration, results in a rate of growth nearly twice that prevailing in the middle of the nineteenth century.' The details of growth vary from territory to territory: Trinidad and British Guiana have experienced greater natural increases than other islands because of their large population of East Indian origin. Aggravating this pressure on resources there have been natural disasters—floods and hurricanes—which have caused unemployment and poverty.

The second main cause of recent migration, linked with the first, is the high level of unemployment and under-employment in the West Indian territories. The general low level of wages and the lack of opportunity have caused West Indians to look outside their islands for economic improvement.

Thirdly, doors to other countries have been closed. The 1952 McCarran–Walter Act reduced the flow of West Indians to the United States of America to a mere trickle, and entries to other countries on the American continent, previously open to West Indian migrants, have also been made more difficult.[2]

It would be foolish to deny the importance of the factors that Mrs. Glass lists, but it is necessary, for a correct understanding of this migration, to show that they are passive and not dynamic. They are some of the factors that allow migration to take place: they are not the factors that directly stimulate it. To show that this is so, one must make first, a brief analogy with previous migrations from the West Indies; secondly, a detailed comparison of

[1] Glass, op. cit., pp. 6–7.   [2] Ibid.

the rates of population growth and so on, with rates of emigration, which show that these factors are not correlated; thirdly, an analysis of the 'pull' factors, that shows that these were the real dynamic of the movement.

The previous largest emigration from the West Indies took place mainly in the period 1881 to 1921. Indeed, in the period up to 1881, the migratory movements had been almost wholly into the region and within it and the general preoccupation had been with the problem of expanding the working population. Deprived of the possibility of direct importations of slaves, with the cessation of the slave trade in 1807–8, the planters turned to their own slaves as the best way of increasing their numbers. Incentives were offered to increase the birth-rate.[1] In addition, marriage was forbidden for the slaves in the hope that this would encourage promiscuity and that this, in turn, would increase the birth-rate. With the abolition of slavery in 1834, there was a considerable movement of emancipated labour from the estates. Considerable numbers, it is true, moved to work on sugar estates in Trinidad and British Guiana, which had developed much later than the others, but with the abolition of the slave trade and the later abolition of slavery, there was a reluctance to do estate work and a consequent shortage of labour. In 1838, four years after the Emancipation, the second largest immigration movement to affect the West Indies began. It was of indentured Indians and their families and continued until 1917. The territories most affected were British Guiana and Trinidad.

British Guiana	238,900 (55·3%)
Trinidad	143,900 (33·3%)
Jamaica	36,400 (8·4%)
Grenada	5,900 (1·4%)
St. Lucia	4,400 (1·0%)
St. Vincent	2,500 (0·6%)
St. Kitts	300 (0·1%)[2]

[1] This and most of the historical demographic material is based on this article: G. W. Roberts, 'Some Demographic Considerations of Federation', *Social and Economic Studies*, Vol. 6, No. 2, 1957, pp. 264–5.

[2] G. W. Roberts, *Population of Jamaica*, p. 128.

Generally speaking, the large emigration movement which took place between 1881 and 1921 is attributed to the contraction of the sugar industry. On reflection, it seems that the increased opportunities outside the West Indies, particularly in the demand for labour to work on the construction of the Panama Canal, was of greater importance. After all, at the same time as the West Indies were experiencing their largest emigration movement up to that time, they were also experiencing their second largest immigration movement. Some authors have assumed that because sugar prices were falling and emigration was taking place, that the movement of East Indian indentured workers also declined in the last quarter of the nineteenth century.[1] In fact, the number of indentured workers rose at this period.[2] Thus the argument that emigration took place at a time that there was lack of internal demand for labour, has serious flaws. It is true that most of the emigration at this time was from Jamaica and that most of the immigration was into Trinidad and British Guiana but this does not alter the argument. It is difficult to postulate a general decline in West Indian sugar to explain emigration from Jamaica while an increase in East Indian immigration into Trinidad and British Guiana, which was dependent on increased demand for labour from the sugar estates, was also taking place.

If the large-scale emigration which took place at this time did not coincide with an internal crisis, it is also true that the major economic crisis which occurred in the late 1920s and the 1930s did not bring about emigration. The inter-censal period 1921–46 overlaps the period of economic depression, and emigration to the U.S.A. and Venezuela continued until 1924 and 1929 respectively, when restrictions were imposed.[3] There were also

[1] G. W. Roberts in *The Economy of the West Indies*, edited by G. E. Cumper, I.S.E.R., Kingston, Jamaica, 1960, p. 28.

[2] I. Ferenczi, *International Migrations*, Vol. 1, edited by W. F. Willcox, National Bureau of Economic Research, New York, 1929, pp. 506–20. East Indian immigration into Trinidad and British Guiana rose from 126,506 from 1850–74 to 166,395 in 1875–99. These are the only territories for which continuous data are available but these two territories accounted for all but 12 per cent of the Indian immigration.

[3] Ferenczi, op. cit., p. 393. Malcolm Proudfoot, *Population Movements in the Caribbean*, Caribbean Commission, Trinidad, 1950, p. 16.

considerable outward movements associated with war work.[1] Nevertheless, taking the period 1921–46 as a whole, there was no net emigration. The depression years produced instead a small net immigration. Roberts estimates that there was an average net inward movement to the West Indies of fifty per year during this period.[2] This period also saw one of the greatest average rates of population growth experienced in the region up to that time: 1·7 per cent per annum.[3]

Thus the conditions which Mrs. Glass considered to be the mainspring of West Indian migration to Great Britain in the 1950s were present *a fortiori* in the preceding period—population growth reached its highest recorded rate up to that time; unemployment had probably never been higher; previously open doors were shut to West Indian emigrants—yet these conditions failed to produce emigration. All these conditions were permissive; the dynamic of demand for labour outside the region was lacking.

A final word should be said about the McCarran–Walter Act as a reason for migration to Britain. It undoubtedly deflected to Britain migrants who would have preferred to have gone to the U.S.A. On the other hand, the scale of the movement to Britain was far larger than any previous West Indian movement to the United States so that it must be seen as more than simply the deviation of an already existing stream.

The analysis put forward by Dr. R. B. Davison of the reasons for West Indian migration to Britain, though different from those advanced by Mrs. Glass, fall into the same category: they are both concerned with 'push' rather than 'pull' factors. Davison pointed out, through an extremely perceptive method, that there was an inverse relationship between the wealth of the West Indian territories, measured in terms of Gross Domestic Product

---

[1] See for example ibid., pp. 17, 21, 22; A. H. Richmond, *Colour Prejudice in Britain*, Routledge and Kegan Paul, London, 1954, p. 23; Sheila Patterson, *Dark Strangers*, Tavistock, London, 1963, pp. 38–9.

[2] G. W. Roberts, 'Prospects for Population Growth in the West Indies', *Social and Economic Studies*, Vol. 11, No. 4, 1962, p. 350.

[3] Cf. 0·24 per cent p.a. 1911–21, 1·02 per cent p.a. 1891–1911, 1·16 per cent p.a. 1881–91, 1·62 per cent p.a. 1871–81.

per capita and the degree of emigration.[1] The statistics that he uses to assess the degree of migration are of doubtful value and incomplete, but his method of analysis is excellent and his conclusion is confirmed, in general, by the only alternative statistics. However, the relationship of wealth to emigration does not make lack of wealth in the West Indies the dynamic of migration. It is still a permissive condition: in poorer territories conditions are more permissive, perhaps, towards emigration, but poverty itself does not give rise to the movement.

It is clear that an accurate assessment of the variation in rates of emigration from the various West Indian territories is basic to any analysis of the importance of internal factors in accounting for these variations. It is therefore at this point that one must come to grips with the problem of evaluating the available statistics of the migration both for the individual territories and for the West Indies as a whole. Readers who wish to omit the detailed examination of these statistics may turn to a summary of some of the main conclusions on page 22.

[1] R. B. Davison, *West Indian Migrants*, Institute of Race Relations, O.U.P., London, 1962, pp. 43–4.

CHAPTER 2

COMPARISON OF MIGRATION FROM THE VARIOUS TERRITORIES

One can speak with a degree of certainty but no complete accuracy about the size of the movement of West Indians to Britain. The statistics on migration kept in the West Indies themselves are of uneven value.[1] First, the amounts of net movement to total arrivals and total departures are small so that small variations or errors in the totals from which they are derived can give large differences in the net figures. Secondly, the islands differ in their methods of classification. Arrivals and departures are classified sometimes according to birth-place, sometimes by nationality, sometimes by place of residence or by proximate or ultimate place of embarkation or disembarkation. The information may be taken from ships' lists or from embarkation or disembarkation cards and there may be different degrees of lag between the actual months of travel and those to which they are ascribed in the records. In the case of Jamaica these figures seem to have a greater degree of reliability than those for most other territories and they have been used as the basis of a careful study by Roberts and Mills of the early years of the movement.[2] Sometimes the figures for other territories are quoted in Colonial Reports and are useful in establishing dates at which the movement became large enough to excite official recognition.[3]

The difficulties that have been noted with West Indian statistics do not lessen when an attempt is made to assess the volume of the movement to the United Kingdom. No one agency in the

[1] E. P. Reubens, *Migration and Development in the West Indies*, I.E.S.R., Kingston, Jamaica, 1961, pp. 19–20.

[2] G. W. Roberts and D. O. Mills, 'Report: Study of External Migration affecting Jamaica, 1953–5', supplement to *Social and Economic Studies*, Vol. 7, No. 2, 1958.

[3] See Appendix 2, p. 108.

West Indies supervised emigration statistics for the whole area
and statistics published in the source area are of very uneven
value, where they exist. Before assessing the position in individual
territories, a comparison of the available figures for total immigration by year into the United Kingdom will be considered.
These figures have all been collected in this country, though in
one case, partially from information sent from the West
Indies.

The first source is the only official enumeration of West
Indian and other commonwealth citizens that the British Government used to undertake prior to July 1962. The figures appear in
the *Annual Abstract of Statistics*.

TABLE 1[1]

Movement direct by Sea of Immigrants and Emigrants between the
United Kingdom and non-European Countries
Immigrants from non-European Countries*

	1954	1955	1956	1957	1958	1959	1960	1961	1962
British West Indies and Bermuda	9·9	11·9	10·5	6·1	7·4	8·8	15·6	18·0	11·3

(thousands)

* By last country of permanent residence—twelve months or more.

The shortcomings of these statistics are many. First, they
include only those persons who travelled direct, by sea, to this
country. It is known that many migrants who travelled by sea
went on Spanish or Italian vessels[2] which debarked them at
continental ports from which they reached England by rail and
short sea crossings. These migrants would not be included in the
official enumeration. Secondly, the figures do not include those
who travelled by air. Flying came to assume a dominant position
in the later years of the movement. In 1960 19,657 migrants from
Jamaica to the U.K. chartered flights while 12,403 travelled by
ship.[3] Figures from the Jamaican Migrant Service's Office in

---

[1] *Annual Abstract of Statistics 1963*, Central Statistical Office, p. 40.
[2] See G. W. Roberts and D. O. Mills, op. cit.; Glass, op. cit., p. 9.
[3] *Colonial Report: Jamaica 1960*, H.M.S.O. London, 1963, p. 141.

London showed 18,441 arrivals in 1962 by air compared with 5,638 by sea (unpublished statistics). Thirdly, persons included in these statistics are not necessarily all West Indians. Fourthly, these figures show a different trend in the period 1955–9 to the Migrant Services Division statistics and the estimates of the British Home Office. These deficiencies make these, the only official statistics, useless for our purposes.

The statistics of the Migrant Services Division and the unofficial estimates of the Home Office are by far the most important sources for analysis. These two sets of figures will be taken together but first a little of their background must be given. The Migrant Services Division of the Commission in the United Kingdom for the West Indies, British Guiana, and British Honduras was established in December 1958, extending and taking over the functions of the British Caribbean Welfare Service which, in 1956, had taken over from a Jamaican civil servant seconded to Britain for duties as a welfare liaison officer.[1] The Migrant Services Division, was itself truncated by the break-up of the West Indies Federation and in June 1962 became the Jamaican Migrant Services Office.

Under its various titles one of the main jobs of the Division remained the same—meeting groups of West Indian immigrants when they arrived in Britain. The Division was informed of the dates, numbers, and place of arrival by the local authorities in the West Indies. They also received information on numbers from couriers with the parties. The Migrant Services Division figures therefore refer to migrants travelling in organized parties.

There are two main reservations about the M.S.D. statistics. First, since the Division met only the organized parties, individual travellers or small, unorganized groups would not be met and would not be included in M.S.D. statistics for arrivals. These statistics therefore underestimate arrivals. Secondly, in the period before all organized parties were met, the figures for arrivals are low when compared with the figures for departure from Jamaica given by Roberts and Mills.

[1] Glass, op. cit., pp. 8–9.

TABLE 2

Figures for Arrivals from Jamaica

	1953	1954	1955
Permanent emigration to the U.K. from Jamaica	2,159	8,039	27,253
Movement to U.K. on holiday, business, or study from Jamaica	1,070	1,203	1,532
Total movement to U.K. from Jamaica from Roberts and Mills' figures	3,229	9,242	28,785
Total arrivals from Jamaica, M.S.D. figures	1,750	8,775	17,895

Source: Based on tables 4C, 4E, and 4F in G. W. Roberts and D. O. Mills, op. cit., and 'Statistical Tables, West Indian Migrant Arrivals in the United Kingdom, 1953–1960', duplicated and supplied by the M.S.D.

Both these reservations therefore have the same conclusion: M.S.D. figures underestimate arrivals from the West Indies.

Prior to 1 July 1962, all Commonwealth citizens had an unrestricted right of entry to this country and there was no power to question them at United Kingdom ports for any purpose other than to establish their nationality and identity. It was not therefore possible to keep official migration statistics. However, in 1955 the Home Office started to maintain estimates of movement into and out of this country of citizens from the West Indies and from Commonwealth territories in East and West Africa, Asia and the Mediterranean. 'By subtracting the number of those believed to have embarked from the number believed to have arrived, an estimate of "net inward movement" was obtained; and this figure is thought to represent as near an approximation as it is possible to obtain of the number of people remaining here and can thus be regarded as immigrants.'[1] The Home Office did publish figures for West Indian migration before 1955 but the basis of their collection was different from that used after the latter year. The figures represented the estimated number of British citizens from the West Indies who came to Britain in substantial numbers with the intention of remaining here.[2] These figures for

[1] Letter from Nationality Division of the Home Office, 2 October 1962.
[2] Lord Mancroft for the Home Office, *Hansard*, House of Lords, 15 February 1956, cols. 1,038–9.

1952–4 were therefore, like those of the M.S.D., not net immigration but for total arrivals.

Thus the main difference between the figures for arrivals given by the M.S.D. and the Home Office after 1954 is that all persons included in the M.S.D. figures are immigrants but not all immigrants are included, while in the Home Office figures all immigrants are included but not all of those included are immigrants.

The Home Office statistics together with those of the M.S.D. are given in the table below. Also in the M.S.D. column are estimates for 1951 and 1952. These have been taken from other sources.[1]

The M.S.D. figures for West Indian arrivals from 1955 to 1961 are, with one exception, 17 to 21 per cent lower than those of the

TABLE 3

Figures for Arrivals from the West Indies

Year	Total arrivals, M.S.D.	Total arrivals, Home Office	Net inward movement, Home Office
1951	898		
1952	1,281	2,200	
1953	2,285	2,300	
1954	10,261	9,200	
1955	24,473	30,370	27,550
1956	26,441	33,400	29,800
1957	22,473	27,620	23,020
1958	16,511	20,710	15,020
1959	20,397	22,390	16,390
1960	45,706	57,170	49,670
1961	61,749	74,590	66,290

Source: M.S.D. figures from 'Statistical Tables . . . 1953–60', op. cit.; Home Office figures from private communication from the Home Office. The figures for the M.S.D. may vary slightly from those published elsewhere, especially for 1960; cf. Patterson, op. cit., pp. 418–19 gives 52,655 and Davison, op. cit., who gives the latter figure on p. 5 and 46,449 on p. 7, though offers no comment on the discrepancy. The figures given above in the table are based on corrections to the arithmetical errors in the M.S.D. Statistical Tables. Home Office figures for net inward movement, given above, are quoted as total arrivals by Davison, op. cit., p. 5.

[1] The 1951 figure is from Glass op. cit., Table A, p. 5. The 1952 figure is from *Colonial Report, Jamaica 1952*, London, H.M.S.O., 1954, p. 5. Both figures refer to Jamaica and since migration from other islands did not really become established until 1954–5, they do not seriously underestimate West Indian migration at this time.

Home Office, but this is to be expected since the M.S.D. met only organized parties of immigrants, while Home Office figures from 1955 onward are supposed to include all arrivals and departures of West Indians. The Home Office figures, because of their more catholic basis, would be expected to be higher than the more restricted figures of the M.S.D. The trends of both sets are identical, that is, they rise and fall simultaneously. Bearing in mind their independent origins and basis of collection, the two sets are in harmony.

If it is accepted that the M.S.D. statistics underestimate West Indian arrivals, the question arises whether the Home Office figures are too high. On the basis of comparison with fragmentary external evidence, it seems more likely that they, too, are too low. 1955 was the last year covered by Roberts and Mills's survey of Jamaican migration to the U.K.[1] and the first covered by the Home Office estimates. By adding the estimates of emigration to the U.K. in 1955 given in the Colonial Reports for the different territories to that given by Roberts and Mills for Jamaica, one arrives at a figure of about 32,870[2] compared with the Home Office figure of 30,370.

Although the M.S.D. figures are underestimates, they are of great importance since they provide a fairly continuous breakdown by sex and island of origin of the immigrants. The existence of the figures for the sex ratio are important in examining the relationship of social to economic conditions in the movement, but the figures for emigration for each territory are basic in any attempt to assess which factors inside the West Indies have affected migration.

It must be said immediately that the M.S.D. figures relating to the individual territories are less perfect even than those relating to the movement as a whole. Davison doubted the

[1] G. W. Roberts and D. O. Mills, op. cit.
[2] 785 from Dominica; 545 from Grenada; 2,754 from Barbados; 28,785 from Jamaica. The total of 32,869 does not include the unknown 1955 part of the 908 persons who migrated to the U.K. from St. Lucia in 1955 and 1956. It also excludes, of course, migration from those territories for which the Colonial Reports make no mention, though lack of mention is assumed to mean lack of movement. See Appendix 2, p. 108.

validity of using them and attempted instead to assess the degree of emigration on the basis of passports issued.[1] The objections to this method, however, seem even greater. In the first place, statistics for Grenada and Montserrat were not available,[2] so that comparable figures for all the territories were not available. In the second place, the assertion that the number of people holding passports and not using them would be small and likely to remain a fairly constant proportion of the passport issue[3] is also doubtful. The experience of the variation in the use of work vouchers, issued under the Commonwealth Immigrants Act, supports this doubt.[4] Thirdly, the issue of passports would probably be higher in those eastern Caribbean islands where there is a fair amount of local traffic with the French islands than in the more isolated Jamaica.

Taking the figures given by the M.S.D. for each territory they may be compared with the only fragmentary evidence available in the Colonial Reports. These figures are, for the most part, in close agreement. However, since the M.S.D. was notified in advance of the departure of organized parties by the authorities in the territories concerned, the figures are not strictly from independent sources. A further complication is that the M.S.D. figures for the Leeward and Windward islands are given as groups for certain years instead of for individual territories. A discussion of these difficulties and the methods used to calculate the amount of migration from the individual territories is given in Appendix 1.

Using the sum of the M.S.D. statistics for each territory and expressing it as a percentage of its 1960 population the comparative degree to which that territory has been affected by the movement to Britain can be assessed as in Davison's method.[5] (B. Honduras is omitted; no migration figures available.)

From Table 4 it can be seen that migration to the U.K. shows an uneven geographic distribution in its intensity. For Trinidad

[1] R. B. Davison, op. cit., pp. 10–12.   [2] Ibid., p. 37.   [3] Ibid., p. 10.
[4] Ceri Peach, 'West Indian Migration to Britain: The Economic Factors', *Race*, Vol. VII, No. 1, 1965, p. 44.
[5] Davison, op. cit., p. 38.

TABLE 4

Emigrants as Percentage of West Indian Populations

	Population from 1960 census*	Total emigration to U.K. 1955–61†	Emigrants as percentage of population
Jamaica	1,609,814	148,369	9·2
Barbados	232,085	18,741	8·1
Trinidad and Tobago	825,700	9,610	1·2
British Guiana	558,769	7,141	1·3
Leewards	122,920	16,025	13·0
Antigua	54,060	4,687	8·7
Montserrat	12,167	3,835	31·5
St. Kitts– Nevis– Anguilla	56,693	7,503	13·2
Windwards	314,995	27,154	8·6
Dominica	59,479	7,915	13·3
Grenada	88,617	7,663	8·6
St. Lucia	86,194	7,291	8·5
St. Vincent	80,705	4,285	5·3

* Provisional figures.   † Jamaica 1953–61, M.S.D.

and British Guiana it amounts to less than 2 per cent of the 1960 population, while for Montserrat it amounts to nearly one-third. Between these extremes, with migration equalling 8 to 10 per cent of this 1960 population are Jamaica, Barbados, Antigua, Grenada and St. Lucia. St. Kitts and Dominica lie between 13 and 14 per cent while St. Vincent has 5 per cent.

These geographic variations are of primary importance to an analysis of the factors affecting migration. If the rate of population growth or the amount of unemployment, for instance, is the main fact influencing emigration, then the intensity of that factor should show the same geographic distribution in its pattern of intensity as migration.

Having established the relative degree of migration to the U.K. the factors which may have given rise to these differential rates can be examined. Basically there are two groups—the demographic and the economic. A section is devoted to the relationship of each to migration to the U.K.

CHAPTER 3

DEMOGRAPHIC AND ECONOMIC FACTORS

The Relationship of Demographic Factors in the West Indies to Emigration to the United Kingdom.

The demographic aspects of population pressure are of two kinds. The first is the rate of growth, which comprises both actual and natural increase; the second is population density, which may be given as a crude overall rate or in relation to cultivated area.

The first measure of the rate of growth which may be considered is that of inter-censal growth. The region as a whole experienced its highest ever rate of growth, 2·2 per cent in the period 1946–60. The previous high rates of growth were all associated with periods of immigration or of non-emigration while previous periods of low and declining rates of growth were associated with periods of emigration. Thus, the inter-censal period 1946–60 was the first in which both high rates of emigration and high rates of increase occurred simultaneously. It has already been noted that Ruth Glass considered the high rates of growth one of the main factors responsible for West Indian emigration to the U.K. The correlation of rates of inter-censal growth with the degree of migration is therefore of great importance.

It is immediately seen that the highest rates of inter-censal increase are not coincident with the highest rates of emigration to the U.K. The opposite is true: British Guiana with the highest rate of growth has the second lowest rate of emigration; Trinidad and Tobago, with the second highest rate of growth—more than 17 per cent higher than the next highest—has the lowest rate of emigration to the U.K. At the other extreme is Montserrat, where the population has declined during the inter-censal period by over 15 per cent. Here the rate of emigration is the highest. Barbados, with the second lowest rate of increase has, on the

TABLE 5

Migration and the Inter-censal Growth

	Migration to U.K. as a percentage of 1960 population		Inter-censal rate of growth 1946–60*	
Jamaica	9·2		21·86	
Barbados	8·1		19·81	
Trinidad and Tobago	1·2		47·98	
British Guiana	1·3		55·48	
Antigua	8·7 ⎫		29·46 ⎫	
Montserrat	31·5 ⎬ 13·0		−15·18 ⎬ 20·06	
St. Kitts	13·2 ⎭		22·49 ⎭	
Dominica	13·3 ⎫		24·89 ⎫	
Grenada	8·6 ⎬ 8·6		22·42 ⎬ 25·11	
St. Lucia	8·5		22·94	
St. Vincent	5·3 ⎭		30·59 ⎭	

* Jamaica, 1946 estimate.

other hand, the fourth lowest rate of emigration to the U.K. St. Vincent, with the third highest rate of growth has the third lowest rate of emigration to the U.K. Antigua with the fourth highest rate of growth has the fifth highest rate of emigration. Thus it can be said that there is no correlation of high rates of inter-censal growth and high rates of emigration to the U.K.

In fact migration seems to have had a discernible effect on some rates of growth rather than vice versa. The high rates in Trinidad seem partially due to immigration while the decline in Montserrat is certainly due to emigration. The high rate of growth in St. Vincent may owe something to the low rate of emigration to the U.K.

On the other hand the British Guiana rate of growth does not seem to have been materially affected by immigration and has remained high. Barbados' low rate of increase coincides with a low rate of emigration to the U.K. and therefore does not seem to have been caused by it.

Therefore neither a clear cut correlation between the rate of inter-censal increase and the rate of emigration to the U.K. can be postulated nor between the rate of emigration to the U.K. and the inter-censal rate of increase. It is clear, however, that the highest rates of increase do not correlate with the highest rates of emigration. High rates of increase are sometimes found with low rates of emigration and sometimes with higher rates. High rates of inter-censal increase seem inadequate an explanation for emigration to Britain.

The second rate of growth that may be considered is natural increase. Unfortunately no comprehensive primary source of statistics is available and those given in an article by G. W. Roberts[1] have to be used.

TABLE 6
Migration and the Rates of Natural Increase

	Migration to U.K. as percentage of 1960 population	1946–60 rates of natural increase (percentage p.a.)†
Jamaica	9·2	2·34
Barbados	8·1	1·93
Trinidad and Tobago	1·2	2·67
British Guiana*	1·3	N.A.
Antigua	8·7	2·29
Montserrat	31·5	1·74
St Kitts	13·2	2·53
Dominica	13·3	2·42
Grenada	8·6	2·73
St. Lucia	8·5	2·56
St. Vincent	5·3	2·97

* Rates of natural increase not given by Roberts.   † Roberts, op. cit., p. 350.

The relationship which emerges is very much the same in type as that which was observed in the previous table. St. Vincent, surprisingly, with the highest rate of natural increase, has the second lowest rate of emigration, British Guiana being omitted. Trinidad with the third highest rate of increase has the lowest rate of emigration. Grenada with the second highest rate of growth

[1] 'Prospects for Population Growth in the West Indies', *Social and Economic Studies*, Vol. 11, No. 4, 1962, p. 350.

has a mid position in emigration—sixth highest or fifth lowest. St. Lucia with the fourth highest rate of natural increase has the fourth lowest rate of emigration. On the other hand, St. Kitts with the fifth highest rate of growth has the third highest rate of emigration to the U.K. Barbados with the second lowest rate of growth has the third lowest rate of emigration. Montserrat with the lowest rate of natural increase has the highest rate of emigration to the U.K. Thus, no correlation is clear cut. The tendency which seems predominant, however is for those territories with the highest rates of growth to have the lowest rates of emigration to the U.K. while those with the lowest rates of increase have the highest emigration. The exceptions to this tendency on the other hand are so numerous that it is dangerous to put it forward as a proposition. Of the four territories, for which statistics are available, with the highest rates of increase, three are among the lowest in emigration to the U.K. Of the four lowest rates of growth, two are found among the four highest rates of emigration. Thus, high rates of natural increase do not seem to be associated with high rates of emigration.

Since the migrants to Britain are predominantly adults it is possible that the rates of growth at the time when they were

TABLE 7

Rate of Emigration and Rate of Population Increase

	Emigration to U.K. as a percentage of 1960 population	Percentage increase 1921–46
Jamaica	9·2	54·0
Barbados	8·1	23·0
Trinidad and Tobago	1·2	52·5
British Guiana	1·3	24·6
Antigua	8·7	40·3
Montserrat	31·5	18·3
St. Kitts–Nevis–Anguilla	13·2	21·0
Dominica	13·3	28·5
Grenada	8·6	9·2
St. Lucia	8·5	36·1
St. Vincent	5·3	38·7

born may have some influence on the degree of emigration. The rates of emigration are therefore compared with the rate of inter-censal growth 1921-46.

It is clear that there is very little relationship between the two sets of figures. Jamaica has the highest rate of growth 1921-46 and the fourth highest rate of emigration to Britain 1953-61. Trinidad has the second highest rate of growth and the lowest rate of emigration. Grenada has the lowest rate of growth and the sixth highest rate of emigration. No correlation emerges.

The possible connection between density of population and migration may now be considered. Proudfoot, for instance pointed out that agricultural Barbados with a population density of 1,200 per square mile, was grossly overcrowded.[1] He also noted that Barbadians were among the great emigrants of the Caribbean. 'Indeed, the overpopulation of this island is such that no other solution has been envisaged.'[2] These statements were published in 1950 and the density had increased to 1,398 per square mile by 1960—more than twice as high as the next highest density in the British West Indies. Emigration to the U.K. was not only officially encouraged but sponsored recruitment, for instance, by London Transport and long-term loans were available for some migrants. In 1960, for instance the Colonial Report noted that 4,341 persons had left for England: 1,011 or 23 per cent on Government sponsorship.[3] Barbados' was the only government to encourage emigration. Thus, in this case a correlation between emigration to the U.K. and density might have been expected.

There is no correlation between the figures for density and those for emigration. Barbados, in spite of its high density, has only a medium rate of emigration. British Guiana with the lowest (or second lowest, if British Honduras is included) density, has the second lowest rate of emigration. Trinidad with the lowest rate of emigration has a higher density than Jamaica which has a much higher rate of emigration. Grenada and St. Lucia with similar sizes of population and similar rates of emigration has

[1] Proudfoot, op. cit., p. 4.   [2] Ibid., p. 20.
[3] *C. R. Barbados 1960 and 1961*, p. 15.

TABLE 8

Population Density and Migration

	Population 1960*	Area sq. miles	Density	Percentage 1960 population emigrated to U.K.†
Barbados	232,085	166	1,398	8·1
Jamaica	1,609,814	4,411	365	9·2
Trinidad and Tobago	825,700	1,980	417	1·2
Antigua	54,060	108ª	501	8·7
Montserrat	12,167	33	369	31·5
St. Kitts	56,693	155	366	13·2
Dominica	59,479	290	205	13·3
Grenada	88,617	133	666	8·6
St. Lucia	86,194	238	362	8·5
St. Vincent	80,705	150	538	5·3
British Guiana	558,769	83,000	7	1·3
British Honduras	90,505	8,866	10	N.A.

ª Includes Barbuda, 62 sq. miles, and Redonda, 1 sq. mile.

Source: * Provisional Census.   † From M.S.D. figures.

dissimilar densities. Montserrat with a density similar to that of Grenada has a rate of emigration more than three times as high. St. Kitts with a density very similar to that of Jamaica has a rate of emigration half as high again.

Using density of population per cultivated acre, as done by Davison[1] we can agree with his conclusion: 'The simple "Malthusian" explanation that the West Indian migration is due solely, or even principally to population pressure on the *land* cannot be sustained.'[2] The figures for population per acre of cropland are taken direct from Davison's book[3] and they therefore omit British Guiana and British Honduras. Davison's 'migration pressure' was measured by the proportion of the population holding passports and these have been replaced by calculation based on M.S.D. figures.

It may be noted in addition that Dominica, one of the islands that is often considered to have the greatest potential for agricultural development, has the second highest rate of emigration.

[1] Davison, op. cit., p. 42.   [2] Ibid., p. 43 [Davison's italic].   [3] Ibid., p. 42.

TABLE 9

Density of Population per Acre of Cropland and Migration

	Population per acre cropland*	Migration to U.K. as a percentage of 1960 population†
Jamaica	2·4	9·2
Barbados	3·4	8·1
Trinidad and Tobago	2·6	1·2
Dominica	1·4	13·3
Grenada	1·7	8·6
St. Lucia	1·8	8·5
St. Vincent	2·9	5·3
Antigua	3·1	8·7
Montserrat	1·5	31·5
St. Kitts	2·6	13·2

Source: * Davison, op. cit., p. 42 (from 1960 population).   † From M.S.D. figures.

Sometimes referred to as a frontier island one might be tempted to think of this outflow as a retreat from the 'pioneer fringe'.

In concluding this section the findings may be reviewed. First, the rate of increase of population growth has been increasing since the 1921 census and large-scale migration to Britain started in the 1950s. There might appear to be a connection between the two facts. However, the high rates of increase have not been uniformly experienced, nor has the rate of emigration been uniform. Internal comparisons between territories show that those with the highest rates of growth have not had the highest rates of emigration.

Taking the territories as a whole, it can be seen that in the past, high rates of emigration took place against a background of decreasing rates of population growth, and increasing rates of growth, prior to 1946, took place in periods of immigration, or when emigration had largely stopped. Thus, historically there is no precedent in the region for emigration to be associated with increasing rates of growth but rather for increasing rates of growth to be associated with immigration. In the inter-censal period 1946–60, when high and increasing rates of population growth and emigration were found, internal comparison shows that there is no correlation between high rates of growth and high rates of emigration.

Secondly, fluctuations in the annual number of emigrants per territory cannot be explained by demographic conditions at the time when most of the emigrants were born. While emigration shows rapid fluctuations the average birth-rates and rates of natural increase show a notable stability of trend.

Thirdly, there is no correlation to be established between rates of emigration and density of population. This applies both to densities on total area and on cultivated land.

It should be emphasized that the importance of population growth in the area is not underestimated. It is, rather, that it is being examined in a relationship other than that in which it is normally seen. Here it is being examined not *per se* but in order to estimate its significance on the geographical variation in the intensity of emigration to Britain. The importance of the population growth is immense in itself; in its relationship to the rates of emigration it is not dominant.

The Relationship of Economic Factors in the West Indies to Emigration to the United Kingdom

The economic situation in the West Indies can be examined through an analysis of the Gross Domestic Products, employment, and wage situations in all of the territories. Unfortunately the statistics relating to these factors vary considerably in comprehensiveness and quality.

Unemployment was dealt with in the 1946 census of the West Indies and that of 1960. The former is not comprehensive because it does not include Jamaica[1] while most of the information from the latter is not yet available. For the period between the censuses, there are a number of sample surveys and reports, but registers of employed and unemployed persons such as are kept in the U.K. are unknown.

The unemployment figures for Jamaica in the 1943 census and the other British West Indies territories in 1946 are given below.

[1] Jamaica's census was taken in 1943 and not in 1946 with the other territories.

TABLE 10

Employment Figures for West Indies

	Total working force	Percentage unemployed
Jamaica	331,050	26·9
Barbados	72,700	6·8
British Guiana	147,481	2·5
British Honduras	16,386	5·3
Leeward Islands	48,684	5·0
Trinidad and Tobago	218,784	7·0
Windwards	105,940	7·1

Source: Jamaica—1943 Census; others—Census of B.W.I., 1946.

There is a remarkable disparity between the percentage of unemployed for Jamaica and the other territories. This is partially explained by the fact that the Jamaican census was taken at the end of 1942 when the economy was depressed through wartime restrictions[1] and also because the Jamaican census was taken in December, which is outside the time of the main agricultural activity, while the 1946 census was taken in April—a month of high employment. Nevertheless it seems that Jamaican unemployment figures were much higher than elsewhere. British Guiana has low figures, but those of the other territories are high by British standards, especially as they were taken at a time of high employment.

For the later period only the figures for Jamaica, Trinidad, and Barbados are available together with qualitative remarks about conditions in other territories. The 1960 census figures were not available at the time of writing, but the *Five Year Independence Plan*, 1963–8, for Jamaica[2] revealed some of the statistics from the census and compared them with a labour force sample survey of 1957.

In the 1957 survey, Jamaican unemployment stood at 18·5 per cent; in the 1960 census at 12·7 per cent.[3] This seems to

[1] G. E. Cumper in 'The Economy of the West Indies', *Social and Economic Studies*, 1960, p. 165.

[2] Government Publisher, Kingston, Jamaica, 1963.

[3] *Five Year Independence Plan*, op. cit., p. 33.

indicate a downward movement in unemployment from the 1942 figure of 26·9 per cent.

There are, however, a number of difficulties in interpreting the figures. The 1957 survey was conducted in August which is usually a month of low employment while the 1960 census was taken in April which usually has high employment in the sugar industry, tourism, and the food-processing industries which employ substantial numbers of female workers.[1] It is estimated that if the 1960 census had been taken in August, unemployment would have been between 92,000 and 94,000 instead of 82,000.[2] This would have given a level of unemployment of between 14·2 per cent and 14·5 per cent. Thus while the readjusted figures for Jamaica still show a substantial level of unemployment, they show also an improvement since 1942 and 1957.

The improvement in the unemployment situation was not due entirely to improvements in the economic condition of the island. While the population aged 15 years and over increased from 894,000 in 1957 to 945,000 in 1960, the number of that group engaged in the labour force declined by 2,000, from 650,000 to 648,000. The nature of this change can be seen from these figures.

TABLE 11

Employment Situation, 1957 and 1960

	April 1960			August 1957		
	Male	Female	Total	Male	Female	Total
			(thousands)			
Population 15 years+	440	504	944*	409	484	893‡
Total labour force	397	251	648	370	280	650
Employed	362	204	566	329	201	530
Unemployed	35	47	82	41	78	129§
Population 15+ outside labour force	43	253	296†	39	204	243

Five Year Plan gives, * 945, † 297, ‡ 484, § 130.

Source: See note [2] below.

[1] Ibid., p. 32. [2] Ibid., p. 33.

From this it can be seen that while employment rose by 36,000 from 1957 to 1960, only 3,000 of this was accounted for by women. While unemployment dropped by 37,000, women accounted for 31,000 of this decrease. While the labour force as a whole declined by 2,000 the male labour force increased by 27,000 and the female labour force decreased by 29,000. While the proportion of males 15 years and over who participated in the labour force remained constant at 90 per cent the female participation dropped from 58 per cent to 50 per cent. Adult emigration in this period is reckoned at 35,000.[1] Thus, the increase in the number employed and the decrease in unemployment is due partly to an increase in the number of jobs, partly to the withdrawal of female labour and partly to emigration.

Unemployment certainly decreased between 1957 and 1960 but this reduction was not caused by exporting the unemployed. They were probably over-represented among the emigrants (Davison's sample shows 19 per cent of the emigrant men and 27 per cent of the emigrant women in 1961 were unemployed compared with figures of 10 and 19 per cent respectively in the 1960 working population of Jamaica).[2] However, the number of new jobs and the decrease in unemployment exceeded the number of emigrants. Between 1957 and 1960, the male employed population increased by 33,000 and male unemployment decreased by 6,000—a net improvement of 27,000. However, only 20,000 men left the island during this period so that there was a combined improvement in the employment situation of 7,000 over and above the male emigration. Between 1957 and 1960 there was a decrease of 31,000 in unemployed women and an increase of 3,000 in female employment—a net improvement of 29,000. Female emigration to the U.K. at this time was 15,000. Thus, the reduction in unemployment was certainly not the result of exporting the unemployed to the U.K. This large decrease in female unemployment seems to indicate that women no longer felt the same need to look for employment as they did

[1] *Five Year Independence Plan*, op. cit., p. 32.
[2] Davison, op. cit., p. 21.

before and this suggests an improvement in the economic conditions of the population of Jamaica at large.

Unemployment in Jamaica was certainly high at the time of emigration, but emigration took place against a background of economic improvement. In the 1930s, while unemployment was at its worst, there was no net emigration. While Jamaica had one of the world's highest rates of economic growth between 1953 and 1962,[1] it also experienced its highest rate of emigration. Thus, the view that explains emigration in terms of unemployment in Jamaica fails to explain why emigration rates were not at their highest at the time of most acute unemployment and why they rose while unemployment decreased. Coupled with the lack of correlation between high population growth and high rates of emigration, it throws doubt on the ability of internal factors to provide a convincing explanation of the emigration.

The data on unemployment in the other territories showed that in 1946 the level was much lower than that for Jamaica in 1943. That position seems to have been maintained. The desperate poverty of West Kingston and parts of Port of Spain in Trinidad do not seem to be found, paradoxically, in the poorer islands. However, while successive investigations have shown successive drops in the unemployment of Jamaica, the same is not true of the other islands, including Trinidad. Cumper notes that between 85 and 95 per cent of males 15 years and over were employed in 1946, but that 'later surveys . . . have shown a decline from the 1946 level—slight in Trinidad (to 83·5 per cent) but very considerable in Barbados (74·7 per cent in crop, 1955) and Antigua (74·6 per cent in crop, 1950).'[2]

The position in Barbados in 1955 was particularly grave according to the account given by Cumper.[3] It may seem significant that though he had not planned to do so, he felt obliged to make a sample study of emigrants to the U.K. as

---

[1] Gene Tidrick, 'Some Aspects of Jamaican Emigration to the United Kingdom 1953–62', *Social and Economic Studies*, Vol. 15, No. 1, 1966.

[2] Cumper, op. cit., p. 166.

[3] G. E. Cumper, 'Employment in Barbados', *Social and Economic Studies*, Vol. 8, No. 2, 1959.

part of his examination of the labour force.[1] Thus it may appear
that high unemployment and emigration occurred at the same
time in Barbados. The survey showed, however, that 70 per cent
of the men and 40 per cent of the women were in skilled trades—
'and there is no definite indication that the emigrants had been
drawn in disproportionate numbers from the unemployed.'[2] It
appears that in late 1955 employers were complaining that
shortages in certain skilled occupation had grown worse since
emigration had begun. Therefore it may appear that while emigration began during a period of high unemployment it already
showed signs in 1955 of giving rise to labour shortages.

The skilled sectors of employment seem to have been most
affected by emigration and in many islands there is a shortage of
labour. In Montserrat, Carleen O'Loughlin reported that skilled
mechanics were as rare as Esquimos.[3] This island has apparently
passed, in five years, from chronic underemployment to shortage
of labour in most areas of the economy.[4] Indeed, the situation in
Montserrat and Nevis, for instance, seems so serious that unless
a plan is put into operation soon there may be no one left for
whom to plan.[5] In Dominica, Dr. O'Loughlin states that labour
limitations enhanced by migration are setting bounds to economic
growth already.[6] In Antigua, the development of the tourist
trade seems to have produced the same shortage in almost the
opposite way. Davison also notes that 'there is now reported to
be a fairly acute labour shortage in Dominica'.[7] The position in
the Leewards and Windwards is best summarized in O'Loughlin's
words; 'It is extraordinary . . . how quickly a position of chronic
underemployment can change to one of labour shortage . . . on
a wide area of the economy through the agency of migration,
as in Montserrat, Dominca, and St. Kitts–Nevis, or through even
a mild injection of capital, as in Antigua.'[8] Since migration has
been taking place from those islands for a shorter time than from

[1] 'Employment in Barbados', p. 128.   [2] Ibid., p. 129.
[3] Carleen O'Loughlin, 'Economic Problems of the Smaller West Indies
Islands', *Social and Economic Studies*, Vol. 11, No. 1, 1962, p. 45.
[4] Ibid.   [5] Ibid.   [6] Ibid.
[7] Davison, op. cit., p. 22.   [8] O'Loughlin, op. cit., p. 46.

Jamaica and has produced much more acute labour shortages one must suppose that the employment situation was originally better too. Thus, if one were to summarize the situation of employment, in the smaller islands, in relation to migration one might conclude that unemployment and underemployment stimulated or allowed migration to begin in the first place, but that it has continued since then in spite of the improved situation.

There are no comparative statistics of wages in the West Indies and Great Britain. It is assumed that their real level is much higher in Britain. Davison suggests that persons remaining in the West Indies and comparing their rates of pay and standards of living with those who have gone to Britain have produced pressure to raise wages in the West Indies.[1] This supports the view that there is a real difference between the two.

However, of the two factors, higher wages or continuity of employment, the latter seems the more important in determining migration. Davison's sample were almost unanimous in giving employment as their reason for emigrating to Britain.[2] It is true, however, that seeking higher wages was not put forward as an alternative question to seeking employment on the questionnaire. Reubens, in his investigation of immigration from the West Indies into Trinidad stated that immigrants 'placed more emphasis on the employment outlook than on wage differentials, which suggests that if jobs were available in the small islands, even at lower wages than Trinidad, many persons would prefer to stay home. . . .'[3] The one qualification that would be made to this statement is that the jobs on the home island should be non-agricultural. Proudfoot also stresses that migration in the Caribbean has always been very closely interrelated with the labour market.[4]

Employment therefore seems to be of great importance to emigrants; intensity of emigration, however, does not seem to be influenced by the geographical variations in employment nor does increasing emigration reflect a worsening labour situation. The disparity noted in the employment situation between Jamaica

[1] Davison, op. cit., p. 52.   [2] Ibid., p. 36.
[3] Reubens, op. cit., p. 5.   [4] Proudfoot, op. cit., p. 8.

and the other territories in the 1940s seems to have continued: Jamaica still has high unemployment while many of the smaller territories have labour shortages. Jamaica remains mid-way in the scale of intensity of emigration and many of the territories with labour shortages such as Dominica, have much higher rates of emigration. Emigration is certainly the cause of labour shortages in many islands. However, while labour shortages have increased inversely to emigration in these cases, they have not thereby halted it. The largest numbers of emigrants in all territories have left in the 1960-2 period when the labour shortage was *ipso facto* greatest.

The shortages of labour are selective, it is true. The shortage of skilled labour is the first to be felt. Therefore it seems that skilled labour is disproportionately affected by migration. On the other hand the Jamaican figures suggest that the unemployed were over-represented among the emigrants as compared with the population as a whole.

It is not known what proportion of the Jamaican emigrants were skilled. Davison makes it clear that the respondents to his questionnaire exaggerated so much that this measurement was impossible.[1] It seems reasonable to assume, however, that while both skilled and unemployed men were over-represented among the migrants, the skilled were most acutely affected. While skilled men have vanished completely from some islands, poverty and unemployment have remained.

As Paget has pointed out, it seems that those who have moved are not always those who needed most to move and conversely those who needed most are not necessarily the ones who have been able to move.[2] The rich islands—Trinidad and Jamaica with their cardboard-and-tin hovelled shanty town sections in Port-of-Spain and Kingston demonstrate this point most clearly, though in St. Vincent Paget notes that officials speak of 'unemployables'.[3]

While unemployment has been proportionately less affected

[1] Davison, op. cit., p. 21.
[2] Verbal communication.
[3] Ibid.

than skilled occupations by emigration they were over-represented in Davison's Jamaican emigrant sample. The explanation
seems to be that emigrants and the unemployed are predominantly young. 64 per cent of the 1957 unemployed in the
Labour Survey were between 15 and 29 years old. 61 per cent of
the men were in this age group and 65 per cent of the women. The
fact that women accounted for 65 per cent of the total unemployed did not, however, give them the larger percentage of
emigrants though the percentage of unemployed women was
higher among Davison's emigrant women than men.[1, 2] The
indications were that the 1960 census would show that young
people and women were still the ones most affected by unemployment.[3]

Thus, while the employment situation is of great importance
to emigrants from the West Indies the geographical variations
in the intensity of emigration to Britain show no correlation with
the geographical distribution of intensity of unemployment. Nor
do the annual fluctuations in the amount of emigration reflect an
annual worsening or bettering of the unemployment situation
in any but an inverse way: the more that emigrate the greater the
demand for labour. Great importance may be ascribed to the
labour situation but it is a passive or permissive importance: it is
not the 'push': it is not the motor of the temporal and geographic
variations in emigration to Britain.

The economy of the islands is more comprehensively recorded
in the figures for Gross Domestic Products, than in employment
statistics. Here, at least there are comparable statistics for the
various territories though unfortunately not for British Honduras.
1957 is the latest date for which comparative figures for the
islands are available. These will be expressed *per capita* and compared with the index of emigration to the U.K.

When Davison made the original calculation (on which this
one is based) comparing his emigration statistics drawn from

[1] See Davison, op. cit., p. 21.
[2] All percentage on employment calculated from figures given in *Five Year
Plan*, op. cit., p. 35.
[3] *Five Year Plan*, op. cit., p. 35.

passport statistics with G.D.P. *per capita*, he concluded the 'relationship which emerges here is quite unmistakable; the higher the national income per head the lower the migration pressure.'[1] The present figures do not show this clear-cut picture, nor in fact did Davison's, since his figures were not strictly-speaking comparable. He had no figures for passports for Grenada or for

TABLE 12

G.D.P. per capita *in 1957 and Emigration*

	1957 G.D.P. at factor cost per capita B.W.I.*	Emigration to U.K. as a percentage of 1960 population
Trinidad and Tobago	822	1·2
Jamaica	572	9·2
British Guiana	455	1·3
Barbados	443	8·1
St. Kitts–Nevis	282	13·2
Antigua	290	8·7
Montserrat	203	31·5
Windward Islands	258	8·6

* *Source: National Incomes Statistics No. 1, 1960*, Federal Statistical Office, p. 20; *B.G. Quarterly Statistical Digest 1961*, p. 9.

Montserrat[2] therefore no comparison was possible for the Windwards as a whole nor for Montserrat. These figures and those for British Guiana have also been included in the table above.

Nevertheless, there seems to be a general accordance with Davison's conclusion. At the extremes Trinidad has the highest G.D.P. *per capita* and the lowest rate of emigration to the U.K.; Montserrat has the lowest G.D.P. *per capita* and the highest rate of emigration. Between the extremes, British Guiana has the third highest G.D.P. *per capita* and the second lowest rate of emigration; Barbados has the fourth highest G.D.P. *per capita* and the third lowest rate of emigration: Antigua and St. Kitts have respectively fifth and sixth highest G.D.P. *per capita* and fifth and seventh lowest rates of emigration.

[1] Davison, op. cit., p. 44.　　　　[2] Ibid., Table 21, p. 38.

Exceptions to this rule are Jamaica, which has the second highest G.D.P. *per capita* and a high rate of emigration, and the Windward Islands which have a low G.D.P. *per capita* and a low rate of emigration to the U.K. The situation in the Windwards seems partly due to the fact that there is a fair amount of movement into Trinidad which possibly reduces the apparent force of migration. On the other hand, if the Leewards were given as a group it is possible that their G.D.P. *per capita* would be lower than that of the Windwards while their rate of emigration was higher. This is true if the 1954 figures for G.D.P. *per capita* are taken in which the Leewards are classed together as a group.

TABLE 13

G.D.P. per capita *in 1954 and Emigration*

	1954 G.D.P. per capita	Emigration to the U.K. as a percentage of 1960 population
Trinidad	596	1·2
British Guiana	401	1·3
Jamaica	375	9·2
Barbados	319	8·1
Windwards	218	8·6
Leewards	215	13·0

Again Jamaica does not fit in with Davison's analysis but the other territories do. If the G.D.P. *per capita* figures have not changed relative to one another since 1954, then Davison's hypothesis is of great value: migration to the U.K. is generally in inverse proportion to the G.D.P. *per capita* of the territory. Jamaica, however, remains a weighty exception to the rule.

The question of the annual fluctuations in numbers migrating to Britain can now be examined against the economic situation in the various territories. Since the intensity of total migration is possibly influenced by the G.D.P. it is necessary to see whether the annual fluctuations of the G.D.P. influence the fluctuations in the number of migrants.

TABLE 14

Percentage Growth of G.D.P. and U.K. Emigration

	Jamaica		Trinidad and Tobago		Barbados		Antigua		Montserrat		St. Kitts	
	Per cent growth of G.D.P.	U.K. Emig.	Per cent growth of G.D.P.	U.K. Emig.	Per cent growth of G.D.P.	U.K. Emig.	Per cent growth of G.D.P.	U.K. Emig.	Per cent growth of G.D.P.	U.K. Emig.	Per cent growth of G.D.P.	U.K. Emig.
1951	16·6		N.A.		13·6							
1952	16·3	1,293	9·4		3·6							
1953	12·3	1,270	12·5		9·7							
1954	12·2	8,000	6·5		0·7		-11·6		8·3		4·4	
1955	14·0	17,895	16·0	771	15·1	2,048	15·9	561*	0·0	523*	2·8	1,049*
1956	16·2	16,098	16·7	1,323*	3·2	2,407*	14·7	598*	-3·8	557*	6·2	1,120*
1957	21·2	13,759	15·8	1,281	22·6	2,112	12·0	641	16·0	561	4·5	779
1958	3·9	10,137	10·9	939	6·9	1,147	7·1	422	0·0	323		928
1959	5·2	12,573	N.A.	973	N.A.	1,514	16·9	353	6·9	455		777

* Computed.

Source: Jamaica and Trinidad from *National Income Statistics*, No. 1, Federal Statistical Office, Trinidad, 1960, p. 20. Others from C. O'Loughlin, *Social and Economic Studies*, Vol. 10, No. 3, 1961, p. 247.

This table summarizes the position as far as it is available. In ten out of twenty-three times migration and growth trends move in opposite directions. If the computed figures for migration for various islands are omitted, then four out of thirteen times the trends move contrarily. Jamaica is the only territory for which continuous records are available of both the rate of growth and emigration and in three times out of seven the trends were not the same. This limited evidence does not suggest that the rate of growth of the economies of the islands affects the annual fluctuations in emigration to the U.K.

If the movements of the economies in relation to one another are examined it can be seen that they do not rise and fall at the same time:

TABLE 15

Economies of the West Indies, 1952–9

	Jamaica	Trinidad and Tobago	Barbados	Antigua	Montserrat	St. Kitts	Total rose	fell
1952	fell	N.A.	fell	N.A.	N.A.	N.A.	—	2
1953	fell	rose	rose	N.A.	N.A.	N.A.	2	1
1954	fell	fell	fell	N.A.	N.A.	N.A.	—	3
1955	rose	rose	rose	rose	fell	fell	4	2
1956	rose	rose	fell	fell	fell	rose	3	3
1957	rose	fell	rose	fell	rose	fell	3	3
1958	fell	fell	fell	fell	fell	N.A.	—	5
1959	rose	N.A.	N.A.	rose	rose	N.A.	3	—

Source: Table 14 above.

If the majority number is taken as the trend, then 41 per cent of the movements were against it.

Analysis of emigration from the islands each year shows a high degree of unanimity. In ten cases out of sixty-six there were movements out of trend. If we omit the computed figures, then eight times out of forty-eight. This gives us 85 per cent or 83 per cent agreement of trend respectively.

Thus, it may be concluded that, while migration pressure is possibly inversely related to G.D.P. *per capita*, annual fluctuations

TABLE 16

Emigration from the West Indies, 1952–61

	1956	1957	1958	1959	1960	1961
Jamaica	fell	fell	fell	rose	rose	rose
Barbados	rose★	fell★	fell	rose	rose	rose
Trinidad	rose★	fell★	fell	rose	rose	rose
B. Guiana	rose★	fell★	rose	rose	rose	rose
Antigua	rose★	fell★	fell	fell	rose	rose
Montserrat	rose★	rose★	fell	rose	rose	rose
St. Kitts	rose★	fell★	rose	fell	rose	fell
Dominica	rose★	fell★	fell	rose	rose	fell
Grenada	rose★	fell★	fell	fell	rose	rose
St. Lucia	rose★	fell★	fell	rose	rose	rose
St. Vincent	rose★	rose★	fell	rose	rose	rose

★ From computed figures.

in emigration to the U.K. do not seem to be related to fluctuations in the annual rate of growth of the G.D.P.

The major point which emerges from this study of rates of growth in relation to emigration is that while the individual cycles of growth do not demonstrate any unanimity the figures for migration do. In some territories, too, the lowest rates of growth coincide with the lowest rates of emigration but in others with the highest. The unanimity of emigration trends is crucial: it seems to over-ride the cycles of growth in different economies; it bears no relation to the degree of unemployment. It argues powerfully that trends in migration are governed by factors external to the West Indies.

CHAPTER 4

CONDITIONS IN THE UNITED KINGDOM

The analysis of the preceding chapter has shown that while there is a generally inverse relationship between the Gross Domestic Product *per capita* and emigration to the U.K. from each of the West Indian territories considered, the annual fluctuation in the amount of movement shows little relation to the rate of economic or population growth in those territories. However, the fluctuations in movement show a great unanimity in trend for all the islands concerned.

Since there is no correlation of trend with conditions in the Caribbean it must be presumed that conditions in the U.K. play a dominant controlling role. The close relationship of the employment situation in this country and West Indian immigration was pointed out by Mr. Gaitskell during the Committee stage of the Commonwealth Immigrants Bill, 5 December 1961[1] and elaborated in a personal letter to the author (23 January 1962). He noted that the quarterly figures for West Indians entering the country since 1956 rose and fell in the same way as the quarterly figures for employment vacancies. Annual figures had not shown a steady increase but showed variations according to the economic conditions existing here.

This can be shown by constructing an index of employment for each year and showing it in relation to the number of West Indians entering the country. When the economy is strong the demand for labour increases and the Ministry of Labour's register of unfilled vacancies increases. The labour market is that part of the British economy with which West Indians have the most intimate contact and it is therefore through the unfilled vacancies that the effect of the British economy on West Indian immigration may be gauged most simply and directly. The index of

[1] Official Report, cols. 1171–2.

employment that is taken is the sum of the quarterly figures for unfilled adult vacancies.

TABLE 17

Index of Employment and Immigration, 1956–60

Year	Employment index*	Arrivals from West Indies†
1956	934,111	26,441
1957	725,271	22,473
1958	535,186	16,511
1959	653,120	20,397
1960	848,542	45,706

Source: ★ Ministry of Labour.   † M.S.D.

The employment index declines from 1956 to 1958 and rises from 1958 to 1960. Arrivals from the West Indies show the same fall and rise. Thus it appears that the British economy was the major determinant of the annual fluctuations in West Indian migration in the 1950s.

Chapter 3 has shown that there is a high degree of unanimity in the migration trends of all the West Indian territories from year to year. It can also be shown that West Indian migration as a whole follows the seasonal patterns of the British economy.

There is a 74 per cent correlation of the trends. The rise and fall of the employment index follows a seasonal cycle with the summer quarters higher than the winter quarters. The arrivals showed a similar cyclical pattern, with the second and third or summer quarters having a heavier inflow than the first and fourth quarters. However, the employment index was more often higher in the second quarter than the third while the opposite was true of West Indian arrivals. Thus the divergence in trends in the third quarters of 1957 and 1960 seem due to the lagging of migration behind employment. Arrival figures were lower, in each case, in the first quarter of the year than in the last quarter of the preceding year. The same was true of the employment index in 1957 and 1958 but in 1959 and 1960 it showed a rise at the beginning of the year so that the trends

TABLE 18
Index of Employment and Immigration, 1956–60

Year	Employment index*	W.I. arrivals†
1956		
1st Quarter	257,481	4,768
2nd „	270,414	9,746
3rd „	229,116	8,422
4th „	177,100	3,505
1957		
1st Quarter	169,554	2,211
2nd „	210,070	4,739
3rd „	196,405	8,841
4th „	149,242	6,682
1958		
1st Quarter	145,952	3,448
2nd „	147,497	6,843
3rd „	131,937	4,463
4th „	109,800	1,757
1959		
1st Quarter	128,279	1,516
2nd „	170,376	4,135
3rd „	184,673	7,192
4th „	169,792	7,554
1960		
1st Quarter	182,394	6,106
2nd „	244,376	12,272
3rd „	230,884	16,607
4th „	190,888	10,721

Source: ★ Outstanding Adult Vacancies, Ministry of Labour.   † M.S.D.

differed on these occasions too. If a correlation of a three month lag of West Indian migrants behind the employment index is attempted, there is a 78 per cent instead of 74 per cent agreement. Thus the very close relationship of the seasonal cycles of employment in the U.K. and immigration from the West Indies is apparent.

It can be argued that this correlation is coincidental rather than connected, fortuitous rather than causal or, that if the two phenomena are related, it is through a rather more distant factor—the weather. It can be argued that West Indians prefer to arrive in this country under the milder summer conditions. The work situation also improves with better weather conditions. Therefore, it is not necessarily the improved employment situation which attracts the seasonal upswing in West Indian arrivals. This is the case put forward by Patterson.[1] There is undoubtedly truth in it.[2]

However, it would be wrong to consider this cyclical movement as purely natural. Quarterly figures of male migration from Europe to the U.S.A. from 1869 to 1896 show the same predominance of numbers in the summer quarters that the West Indians show. From 1896 to 1913, however, the seasonal pattern was inverted. Arrivals were higher in the first and fourth quarters and depressed in the second and third.[3] Thus it appears that migrants do not always travel in their greatest numbers in the mildest seasons.

The pattern of West Indian arrivals during 1959 is instructive in evaluating the relative effects of economic and seasonal influences on migration. The June figure for unfilled vacancies was the highest since the September figure in 1957. The September figure in 1959 confirmed the recovery after the 1958 recession and the December seasonal drop was very slight. West Indian arrivals showed a revival in response and, instead of showing the usual seasonal rise and fall showed successive increases. The December quarter of 1959 is unique in having the highest number of arrivals for its year. The comparatively slight drop in the demand for labour coupled with the fact that the previous quarter was the highest in demand for two years united the effects of contemporary demand with the lag from the previous quarter. If Table 18 is examined once more it will be seen that, where the employment index and West Indian arrival trends do not

[1] Patterson, op. cit., p. 44.

[2] See, however, Albert Hyndman, 'The West Indian in London' in *The West Indian comes to England*, edited by S. K. Ruck, Routledge and Kegan Paul, London, 1960, p. 70.

[3] See B. Thomas, *Migration and Economic Growth*, Cambridge, Cambridge University Press, 1954, Table 127, p. 317. This book is essential reading for students of migration.

coincide, there is a lag of three months between the peak of demand and the peak of arrivals. Thus, the relationship between the cyclical pattern of the employment situation in the U.K. and the seasonal pattern seems more than fortuitous.

A priori it may be argued that, since the numbers of West Indian arrivals show such sensitivity to the employment situation in this country, then those who would be most directly affected by it, that is the men, rather than women and children, should show the greatest sensitivity to it. That is to say that when numbers decline the decline of the number of men should be greater than that of the whole; when numbers increase men should increase more than proportionally. Thus, the proportion of men should rise and fall as the totals rise and fall for this proposition to be true.

TABLE 19

Males as Percentage of West Indian Immigrants, 1956–60

	West Indian arrivals	Percentage male
1956	26,441	58·1
1957	22,473	52·7
1958	16,511	46·4
1959	20,397	49·3
1960	45,706	57·3

Source: M.S.D. figures.

The totals for 1956 and 1957 contain respectively 2,488 and 802 unclassified migrants. If these are taken as non-male the proportions for the two years are 53 per cent and 51 per cent respectively.

It can be seen that the proportion of males in the total rose and fell as the total rose and fell. It is possible to deepen the analysis by examining whether what is true of the West Indies as a whole is true of its geographical components.

There are nine occasions on which the proportion of males failed to rise when the total rose or to fall when the total fell. In 1958 Trinidad and St. Kitts were out of trend; in 1959 Trinidad, Antigua, and St. Lucia; in 1960 British Guiana, Antigua, Montserrat, and St. Vincent. There was, nevertheless, a 73 per cent

TABLE 20

Males as Percentage of West Indian Emigrants, 1957–60

	1957		1958		1959		1960	
	Total	% male	Total	% male	Total	% male	Total	% male
Jamaica	13,303	50·5	10,137	44·3	12,573	47·8	29,547	57·8
Barbados	2,032	48·0	1,147	41·2	1,514	47·6	4,340	57·6
Trinidad and Tobago	1,281	55·0	939	55·8	973	47·6	2,041	56·7
British Guiana	251	54·2	513	60·6	760	62·4	1,008	51·5
Antigua	547	58·3	422	43·6	353	45·3	721	44·0
Montserrat	537	50·3	323	44·3	455	46·6	620	40·2
St. Kitts	714	57·0	928	48·6	777	45·4	1,508	50·3
Dominica	984	57·7	577	53·5	1,116	60·8	1,946	61·2
Grenada	854	64·0	680	50·9	594	53·2	1,809	58·2
St. Lucia	671	60·7	541	49·5	970	49·8	1,308	56·0
St. Vincent	515	69·3	304	54·3	1,088	65·3	858	73·5

Source: M.S.D. figures—unclassified figures have been omitted from the calculations.

positive correlation. If the two deviations which were under 1 per cent are excluded, there was a 79 per cent correlation.

The mechanism by which such a sensitive adjustment to economic conditions was maintained is of great interest. It is apparent that would-be migrants in the West Indies must have a fairly accurate indication of conditions in this country. Letters must have played a much more important part than has been generally assumed. Even the seasonal pattern of immigration is coincident with, rather than connected to, the seasonal cycle of demand for labour; the correlation of the annual demand with the annual supply from each of the islands and the proportion of males in that total requires a physical rather than psychic explanation. Telepathic communication of conditions or guesses may be discounted where there is such agreement of trend.

The 1960 Economic Report for Jamaica supports this thesis: 'Throughout the years since the movement started it has proved to be sensitive to conditions in that country and it is likely that reports in letters received here from Jamaicans in the United

Kingdom now represent the main determining factor as far as the level of migration is concerned.'[1]

Davison's own investigation contains information which supports this view. Almost all the persons that were interviewed in his sample of Jamaican emigrants in 1961 had a specific address in England as a destination indicating that they were in communication before leaving.[2]

Cumper's evidence from a sample of Barbadian emigrants in 1955 showed that only 11 out of 384 were making the trip without a contact at the other end.[3] This investigation suggests that most migrants were informed in some way about conditions in the United Kingdom.

It is not necessary that all that information was effective. The view can be taken that there is a solid core of migrants who would come, no matter what the conditions, and that there is a second group that might be called 'floating migrants' in the same way as there are floating voters. It is this second group, which would respond to reports of conditions. The solid core of committed migrants would be predominantly dependants joining established migrants. Davison's sample survey of Jamaican emigrants showed that 72 per cent of the women had their passages paid for by migrants established in England whereas for men it was much less: 39 per cent.[4] Thus, the floating migrants, who would be much more subject to the influence of the British economic climate, would have been predominantly men.

Tables 19 and 20 demonstrate that the proportion of males among West Indian immigrants rose and fell as the total rose and fell. Table 17 demonstrated that the number of West Indian arrivals rose and fell with the rise and fall of the demand for labour. Table 16 in Chapter 3 showed that the migration trends from all the territories in the West Indies showed a high degree of unanimity. Table 18 in this chapter showed that the movement of West Indian migrants into the U.K. showed a close correlation

---

[1] Quoted in Davison, op. cit., p. 59.   [2] Ibid., p. 23.
[3] G. E. Cumper, 'Employment in Barbados', *Social and Economic Studies*, Vol. 8, No. 2, 1959, p. 129.
[4] Davison, op. cit., p. 32.

with the seasonal demand for labour. Thus, it may be concluded that the movement of West Indian migrants to Great Britain showed a sensitivity to economic conditions here not only from quarter to quarter and year to year but from island to island, and in the composition of the migrant body. It may therefore be concluded that the British economy rather than conditions in the Caribbean was the main determinant in the fluctuation of the volume of immigration from that area.

Failure to interpret the effect of the economy on the numbers and composition of West Indian immigration has led to erroneous and incomplete deductions by other writers. In *West Indian Migrants*, Davison virtually ignores the economic influences of the U.K. on West Indian migration.

The oddest analysis and most confused conclusion was that of Ruth Glass. She noted that 'before 1957, the majority of migrants from the West Indies were adult males. But since then, the number of West Indian women and children who came to Britain has increased steadily: in 1957 it was estimated to be equal to that of the male migrants; in 1958 and 1959 more women and children arrived than men'.[1]

This short passage contains not only a confusion of notions but a misrepresentation of fact. In the first place, the idea of proportion and number have been confounded. Mrs. Glass has assumed that if the proportion of women and children has increased then their number has also increased. The present analysis has shown that the opposite case should be expected. Secondly it is untrue that since 1957 the number of West Indian women and children who came to Britain has increased steadily: Glass's own figures, published on the previous page of her book, contradict her statement.

Year	Men	Women	Children	Unclassified	Total
1956	13,921	9,380	652	2,488	26,441
1957	11,412	9,385	874	802	22,473
1958	7,662	7,768	1,081	—	16,511
1959	10,057	8,219	2,121	—	20,397

Source: Glass, op. cit., p. 5.

[1] Glass, op. cit., p. 6.

The number of women and children declined from 10,259 in 1957 to 8,849 in 1958.

The conclusion that Mrs. Glass drew from the fact that women and children predominated among the migrants in 1958 and 1959 was that the West Indians were becoming more settled in Britain.[1] However, the proportion of women and children among the migrants has always been high (over 40 per cent between 1955 and 1964), and, according to this reasoning, they have always been fairly settled. In this conclusion she has shifted the emphasis and inverted the most likely deduction to be drawn from the figures. The increase in the proportion of women and children is unimportant compared with the drop in the total number of immigrants and the decline in the proportion of men. The fact that women and children formed a higher proportion of the total in 1958 and 1959 does not mean that West Indians were becoming more settled: the opposite is true. The decline in numbers below the 1956 level in 1957, 1958, and 1959, and the simultaneous decline of the proportion of men, represents a depressed-economic rather than a settled-domestic state.

Dr. Davison's interpretation of the sex ratio is close to that of Mrs. Glass.

In the Jamaican survey, it was found that the sexes were almost equally represented. . . . The impression gained in the 1961 survey was that the migration had changed its character—the men had gone first, now the women were following them, which suggests that the men concerned were beginning to settle down in Britain with no immediate plans to return permanently to Jamaica.[2]

In fact, it is clear that women following their menfolk represents not a changed but a continuing characteristic of the emigration. There is evidence that this was the case in Barbados in 1955[3] and in Jamaica from 1953–5.[4]

[1] Ibid.
[2] Davison, op. cit., pp. 15–16.
[3] 'Employment in Barbados', p. 129.
[4] G. W. Roberts and D. O. Mills, *The Study of External Migration Affecting Jamaica*, Institute of Social and Economic Research 1958, p. 55.

All of the main commentators refer to the tendency for the movement to grow. Both Glass and Patterson refer to a tendency for the migration to snowball[1] and Davison refers to a ratchet effect.[2] 'The more people who go, the more they encourage others to go.'[3] There is a drawback to these analogies however. Snowballing is a continuous process and the momentum of the 'ratchet effect' 'is likely to be self-perpetuating'.[4] Migration figures, on the other hand, were not ever-increasing. Nevertheless, the general point is clear. The later peaks of migration were higher than the earlier ones. If the numbers were depressed at one stage it seemed that it was only in order to spring to greater heights later. Yet, from the analysis of the figures from 1956 to 1960 it seems that snowballing took place only within a permissive economic situation.

This point is of great importance when the period after 1960 is analysed. 1961 and the first half of 1962, before the enforcement of the Commonwealth Immigrants Act saw a major break with the trend. In 1961 the employment index declined slightly but immigration from the West Indies showed a great increase. In the first two quarters of 1962 it was evident that the economy was depressed to the levels of the first two quarters of 1958 and 1959. Immigration reached the highest recorded rate for those quarters.

TABLE 21

Index of Employment and Immigration, 1960–2

Year		Employment index*	West Indian arrivals†
1960	1st half	426,770	18,378
1960	2nd half	421,772	27,328
1961	1st half	468,929	28,886
1961	2nd half	379,369	34,063
1962	1st half	327,992	31,810

Source: * Ministry of Labour.   † M.S.D. excepting the figure for the first half of 1962 which came from the Home Office.

[1] Glass in an article in *The Times*, 22 November 1961; Patterson, op. cit., p. 43.
[2] Davison, op. cit., p. 8.
[3] Ibid., p. 8.   [4] Ibid.

The annual figures for 1960 and 1961 were:

TABLE 22
Index of Employment and Immigration, 1960 and 1961

Year	Employment index	West Indian arrivals
1960	848,542	45,706
1961	848,298	61,749

The decline in the employment index was rather more substantial than these figures demonstrate. If the figures for Wales, the North and Scottish regions, which had very few West Indian immigrants, are omitted the employment index shows a greater decline:

TABLE 23
Index of Employment, 1956–61, omitting Wales, Scotland and Northern England

1956	1957	1958	1959	1960	1961
808,554	609,336	455,937	594,738	760,481	743,178

It is nevertheless clear that the demand for labour, though showing a minor decline, remained at a higher level in 1961 than for the period 1957 to 1959. It is possible, therefore, that the increase in the number of West Indians was due to the conditions remaining favourable. The size of the increase in migration, however, diminishes the strength of this argument, and the continuation of this high level, in spite of the very depressed demand for labour in the first half of 1962, seems to indicate that a new trend in migration is apparent in this eighteen-month period.

Further proof of this is found in the sex ratio of the migrants in 1961 and the first half of 1962. For the first time since 1955, a rising number of migrants was associated with a declining proportion of males. In 1961 they formed 46·9 per cent of the total compared with 57·3 per cent in 1960. The figures for the first half

B

of 1962 are not directly comparable with these: the ending of the proposed West Indies Federation in 1961 led to the transformation of the Migrant Services Division into the Jamaica Migrant Services Division. Since Jamaicans represent over 60 per cent of the West Indian immigrants and since there is such uniformity of trends between the islands it may be assumed that what is true of the Jamaica figures is true of those for the West Indies.

TABLE 24

Jamaican Immigration: Percentage Male

Year		Total number	Male	Percentage
1959		12,573	6,014	47·8
1960		29,547	17,089	57·8
1961		39,090	18,513	47·4
1962	1st half	19,683	8,416	42·8

Thus, it may be concluded that the movement against the economic trend in 1961 and the beginning of 1962 was caused by a large increase in the number of women and children.

The reason for this increase seems to have been fear of immigration controls in the U.K. Both Davison[1] and Patterson[2] attributed the rise of total numbers in 1961 to fear of restrictive legislation. However, in the period between the second reading of the Immigrants Bill (16 November 1961) and its official enforcement (1 July 1962) the new nature of the movement from the West Indies became overt. It was a rush to beat the ban. Even during this period of 'rush' the six-monthly totals did not vary greatly from those recorded during the last three six-monthly periods (see Table 21). Thus there is evidence that the rush to beat the 'ban' commenced about a year before the official intention to introduce the Commonwealth Immigrants Bill was announced. It is ironic that the large increase in the movement was due to the fear of governmental control, while the Government adduced the need of control from that same large increase.

[1] Davison, op. cit., p. 7.
[2] Patterson, op. cit., p. 43, footnote 1.

The large increase in the proportion of women and children in the expanded number of arrivals during the eighteen-month period prior to the enforcement of the Immigrants Act suggests that the movement was predominantly of dependants. Once again it seems that an increase in the proportion of dependants represents uncertainty rather than stability. The previous analysis showed its connections with depressed numbers and economic depression: the present period shows it connected with increased numbers through political uncertainty.

Paradoxically the break-down of the control of the British economy over West Indian migration reinforces the conclusion that conditions in Britain were the major determinants in the trends of that migration. It shows *not* that the trends were determined elsewhere but that political forces overtook those of economics in the commanding position.

The numbers of West Indians in Britain who returned to the West Indies were among the statistics that were lost when the Migrant Services Division was broken up. The Home Office figures show a continuous, but uneven increase in the numbers returning. It is difficult to know whether these represent migrants who have made money and now want to leave Britain or whether they are those who are leaving because they have not made money. The Colonial Report for Jamaica thought that the relatively large number returning in 1958 reflected the bad employment situation and racial disturbances in Britain.[1] The following year the Colonial Report thought that a large number of those that had returned were on holiday.[2]

On the whole it seems that conditions in Britain influence the proportion of returns to arrivals. The highest proportions were in 1958 and 1959 at the time of the recession. In spite of the continuous increase in numbers returning, from 1958 they formed a decreasing proportion in relation to arrivals.

Thus, both in the movement into Britain and in the outward movement to the Caribbean, West Indian migrants have been largely governed by conditions in this country.

[1] *C.R. Jamaica 1958*, London, H.M.S.O., 1961, p. 125.
[2] *C.R. Jamaica 1959*, London, H.M.S.O., 1962, p. 138.

TABLE 25

Proportion of West Indian Departures to Arrivals, 1956–61

Year	Arrivals	Departures	Proportion
1956	33,400	3,600	1 in 9·3
1957	37,620	4,600	1 in 8·2
1958	20,710	5,690	1 in 3·6
1959	22,390	6,000	1 in 3·7
1960	57,170	7,500	1 in 7·6
1961	74,590	8,300	1 in 9·0

Source: Home Office estimates.

CHAPTER 5

THE EFFECT OF THE COMMONWEALTH IMMIGRANTS ACT AND THE WHITE PAPER, 1965

While it is clear that in the period up to and including 1960 the flow of West Indian migration was favoured by economic conditions, it was equally clear that social conditions acted against immigration. Shortage of manpower encouraged immigration: shortage of housing militated against it. It was as a response to social pressure that the Conservative government introduced the Commonwealth Immigrants legislation in 1961 which came into effect on 1 July 1962.

Under the Act, persons from the Commonwealth wishing to work in the United Kingdom needed work vouchers. Category A was for applicants who had a job to come to in this country; category B was for applicants with skills or qualifications; category C was for those not included under categories A or B. The vouchers were valid for six months and could be extended for up to six months, if good reason were shown.[1]

At the time that the Commonwealth Immigrants Bill was debated it was clear that its purpose was to restrict, not merely to regulate, the movement of Commonwealth immigrants and particularly that from predominantly coloured countries.[2] Because no one wished to avow this intention, it was announced that the issue of vouchers was to be regulated according to

[1] Commonwealth Immigrants Act, Statistics 1963, Cmnd. 2151, p. 10.
[2] Mr. Gaitskell, in opposing the Bill, showed how the West Indian movement was already regulated by economic conditions. *Hansard*, House of Commons, 5 December 1961, cols. 1171–2. He also pointed out that citizens of Eire would be allowed unrestricted entry while colonials, who had identical citizenship as natives of the United Kingdom, would be subject to control. *Hansard*, op. cit., cols. 1172–3.

economic and social conditions in this country.[1] It is clear from the preceding analysis, however, that the movement was already governed by economic conditions in this country. The social conditions, on the other hand, were permanently opposed to immigration. The social conditions which were to be taken into account were housing, pressure on the educational system and social friction in the U.K. It is clear that the attitude of the majority of the population was against coloured immigration;[2] as far as housing was concerned, the country had a permanent shortage and the educational facilities had been chronically overloaded. Thus, the two major terms of reference (social and economic) of the committee of ministers which was to decide the issue of vouchers were irreconcilable in times of economic boom. Economic considerations would favour immigration; social conditions would always be opposed to it. Even the provisions for restrictions in emergency conditions, such as race riots in the U.K. or outbreaks of epidemics abroad, could operate only by delayed action. They would have the effect of an immediate reduction in the issue of vouchers, but the response in immigration might take up to six months. They would have a direct effect on voucher-holders only, not on dependants.

Despite the internal contradictions of applying the Act, the immediate apparent effect was a dramatic decrease in net immigration. In the six months prior to its enforcement, the Home Office estimated a net arrival of 31,810 West Indians in the U.K. In the six months after the Act's enforcement there was a net inflow of 3,241 and in the following six months, 3,641. Figures

[1] For these conditions, see R. B. Davison, *Commonwealth Immigrants*, London, Oxford University Press for the Institute of Race Relations, 1964, p. 10.

[2] Gallup Polls showed that in November 1961, 76 per cent of those asked approved when questioned 'Do you approve or disapprove of the measures that the government intends to take in controlling immigration?', *Political Index*, Report 23, November 1961. In August 1965 when asked 'A strict limitation on the number of immigrants allowed from the Commonwealth is being applied. Do you approve or disapprove?', 87 per cent approved, *Political Index*, Reports 64 and 65, August and September 1965. In August 1965, National Opinion Polls found that 88 per cent of those asked thought the Government right when asked 'Do you think the Government was right or wrong to introduce new measures to restrict immigration?', personal letter dated 3 July 1967.

for Indian and Pakistani immigration show similar contrasts for the periods before and after the Act.

The effect of the Act was therefore taken to mean that immigration was considerably reduced, particularly from the West Indies, India, and Pakistan. This was the view taken by the newspapers,[1] radio, and television.

From the previous analysis, this view seems mistaken. The first effect of the Act came, paradoxically, before the Act was effective. West Indians hurried into the country in a declining economic situation. Demand for labour had fallen off since 1960. Normally, the number of West Indian immigrants would have been expected to decline in the eighteen-month period before 1 July 1962. The Act was a psychological barrier. Dependants, who would have been allowed uncontrolled entry to the country under the legislation, still put forward their date of arrival. Under the depressed economic conditions of 1962, the total net inflow of 35,051 was not unreasonable. It is the unbalanced time of arrival that is significant. Ninety-one per cent arrived in the uncontrolled six months of the first half of the year and 9 per cent in the second. Thus, when commentators pointed to the sudden drop in numbers after 1 July 1962, they were pointing to the wrong side of the fence. The significant fact was the excessively large number before that date.

With the enforcement of the Act, the psychological barrier and political uncertainty were removed and economic determinants resumed their role of controlling numbers and trends. The last two quarters of 1962 had employment indices of 147,074 and 109,663 respectively, as low as those for 1958. This, coupled with the siphoning-off of many migrants into the first half of the year explains the paucity of immigrants after the Act came into effect.

The evidence of the voucher system showed that it was not government control which kept migrants out at this time. In the first year of control, 165,567 applications for vouchers were

[1] For example, see Mark Arnold-Foster, 'Immigration Rope Trick', the *Observer*, 2 June 1963; Colin Legum, 'How the Migrant Act works', the *Observer*, 24 November 1963; *The Times*, 5 October 1963.

received and 44,750 or 27 per cent were successful.[1] Of the vouchers issued, 14,680 were used; 6,315 vouchers were returned either because they were no longer needed or because their validity had expired; 2,450 extensions were granted. Thus, 20 per cent of the vouchers issued had either lapsed or had been extended. Only 33 per cent of those issued had been used. It might appear from the low rate of issue of vouchers that the Government was restricting immigration, but application for vouchers is a poor indication of the ability to migrate. Eighty-five per cent of the applications came from India and Pakistan and reports from those countries suggested that the very high number was due to mistaken ideas about the nature of vouchers. It was apparently widely believed that vouchers entitled the migrants to free passages to the U.K. Application forms for vouchers, under these circumstances had a saleable value and there were many cases of the sanctity of the mails being disregarded.[2] The table below shows that while India and Pakistan submitted a large number of applications for vouchers and received the largest numbers issued (although only a small proportion of those requested) they had the lowest rate of use.

TABLE 26

Issue and Use of Vouchers in First Year of Commonwealth Immigrants Act[3]

	Applications	Vouchers issued	Vouchers used	Percentage used
West Indies	7,260	5,070	2,618	52
Pakistan	82,037	10,734	3,404	32
India	58,920	17,419	3,571	21
Australia	1,715	1,533	795	52
Canada	1,925	1,507	621	41
N. Zealand	504	430	256	60

In the first nine months of the Act's enforcement there were 5,907 applications for vouchers from the West Indies of which

[1] Cmnd. 2151, op. cit., Table 3, p. 11.   [2] The *Observer*, 2 June 1963.
[3] Cmnd. 2151, op. cit., Table 2A, p. 8 and Table 3, p. 11.

73 per cent were successful; of these 2,024 or 47 per cent were used.[1] In the first year of control 7,260 applications were received from the West Indies. 5,070 or 70 per cent were granted and 2,618 or 52 per cent were used.[2] From 1 July 1962 to 25 October 1963, 9,563 applications were received from the West Indies; 5,961 or 62 per cent were granted; 3,358 or 56 per cent were used. Six hundred and sixteen vouchers or 10 per cent of those issued had been returned unused.[3]

Thus, in this period there was a low demand for vouchers, a high but declining rate of issuing them and a low rate of use of those issued. Therefore it was not Government pressure which was reducing the inflow from the West Indies. The low demand for labour which characterized 1962 continued in 1963 and it was this that was responsible for the low number of West Indian arrivals.

The second factor which explains the low net immigration from the West Indies at this time was the high rate of departures to arrivals. In the first year of the Act, 26,040 West Indians arrived and 19,176 left.[4] This proportion of 1 in 1·4 was much higher than the previous highest figure in 1958. The number returning was the highest recorded for a twelve-month period. The figures for previous years are not directly comparable with the twelve-month period, 1 July 1962 to 30 June 1963. However, combining the figures for the periods before and after the introduction of the Act, the large rise in the numbers returning can be seen. The total figure of 16,979 for 1962 was double the previous highest figure of 8,300 in 1961 (see Table 25, Chapter 4).

The statistics for the first year of the Act show that there was a net outflow of 468 West Indian men from the U.K. compared with a net inflow of 3,716 women and 3,157 children.[5] There are no comparable figures for the proportions of males, females, and children returning to the West Indies before the Act. With

[1] From figures given in written answers, *Hansard*, 6 May 1963, cols. 12–14; *Hansard*, 13 May 1963, cols. 126–8.

[2] More accurately 13½ months, since vouchers were applied for and issued from mid-May 1962; Cmnd. 2151, p. 10.

[3] From figures given in written answers, *Hansard*, 26 November 1963, cols. 55–6.

[4] Cmnd. 2151, Table 1A, p. 5.   [5] Ibid.

the decrease in total numbers, the proportion of males decreased too. The net outflow of men, their declining proportion among the diminishing number of arrivals, the low proportion of voucher-holders arriving in the U.K. all suggest that it was the economic conditions which were governing the flow of migrants. The large and sudden increase in the number and proportion of returning West Indians suggests that this was an overflow from the excessive number of arrivals before the Act at a time of declining demand for labour.

Viewed against the pattern of immigration from the rest of the Commonwealth, the thesis of the nature of the controls on the movement into the U.K. is even clearer. Taking the West Indies, India, and Pakistan, the estimates of the annual net movement are:

TABLE 27

Net Inward Movement from India, Pakistan, and West Indies

	1957	*1958*	*1959*	*1960*	*1961*	*1962*
India	6,600	6,200	2,900	5,800	23,750	22,550
Pakistan	5,200	4,700	900	2,500	25,100	24,943
W. Indies	23,000	15,000	16,400	49,700	66,300	35,051

Source: Hansard, 1 December 1961 for 1957–60. Home Office monthly estimates January 1961 to June 1962 and Home Office official returns for July to December 1962.

The Indian and Pakistani movements appear to have been in the pioneer stage from 1957 until 1960. Their numbers were small and the response to economic stimuli was more sluggish. Though the bottom of the economic depression was reached in 1958, the net inflow of Pakistanis and Indians did not reach a corresponding trough until 1959. In 1961 fear of control quadrupled the Indian net inflow and the Pakistani figures rose ten-fold. 1962 showed only a slight decline but the figures before and after the implementation of control are dramatic. In the first six months of 1962 there was a net inflow of 19,050 Indians; in the second six months, 3,500. In the first six months there was a net inflow of 25,080 Pakistanis: in the second six months there was a net outflow of 137. The strain of the high rate of arrivals before the Act became evident after July.

Events after July 1962 showed that Government action was not responsible for the decrease in immigration during the first year of control. The small proportion of vouchers issued to vouchers requested might suggest a barrier to immigration: the low proportion used of this low proportion issued suggests the opposite. If Government action alone were responsible, a high proportion of the vouchers issued would have been used. As it was, not only were they not used but a significant proportion had expired.[1] The countries that showed the greatest demand used only a small fraction of the vouchers issued.

The real reason for the decline in the net inflow was two-fold. First, the decline in the demand for labour decreased the number of arrivals. Secondly, the strain of the large number of arrivals at a time of low demand for labour before the enforcement of the Act gave rise to a very high rate of return, a backwash which became evident after June 1962.

The fact that it was economic conditions and not the enforcement of the Act that accounted for the sharp decrease in immigration in the first year of the Act's enforcement must have become clear to the Government by the middle of 1964. Demand for labour showed a continuous recovery from 1962 to 1965 and with it, immigration increased.

TABLE 28

Demand for Labour, 1962–5

Year	Labour demand index
1962	584,729
1963	593,322
1964	913,964
1965	1,076,316

Source: Ministry of Labour Gazette.

[1] The only statistics which distinguish the countries of origin of unused vouchers show that up to 25 October 1963, 11,986 had been returned of which 10,489 came from India and Pakistan. (Written answer in *Hansard*, House of Commons, 26 November 1963, cols. 55–6.)

However, while there was a continuous *increase* in demand for
labour from 1962 to 1965, there was a continuous *decrease* in the
number of vouchers issued. This can be seen more clearly if the
figures for the last six months of 1962 are doubled and treated as
if they were for the whole year. On this basis, the *rate* of issue of
vouchers was:

1962	51,000
1963	41,000
1964	21,000
1965	16,000

As a consequence of this reduction and the continuous increase
in the demand for labour, there was an increase in the rate of use
of the vouchers.

TABLE 29

Work Vouchers 1962–5: Commonwealth

Year	Vouchers issued	Vouchers used	Percentage used
1962 (July–Dec.)	25,390	5,121	20
1963	41,101	30,125	73
1964	20,824	14,605	70
1965	16,046	12,880	80

Source: Cmnd. 2979, 1966; Cmnd. 2658, 1965; Cmnd. 2379, 1964; Cmnd.
2151, 1963.

The rate of use was not continuously increasing. It was slightly
higher in 1963 than 1964 but this is probably accounted for by the
backlog of voucher-holders from 1962, when only a small proportion of the vouchers was used. The holders of these vouchers
probably wanted to use them before their validity expired and
were encouraged to do so by the improved economic conditions
of 1963.

The pattern of use of vouchers by the West Indies is similar
to that of the Commonwealth as a whole, though less volatile
because they had been closely attuned to British conditions for a
long period.

TABLE 30

Work Vouchers 1962–5: West Indies

Year	Vouchers issued	Vouchers used	Percentage used
1962 (July–Dec.)	3,068	1,600	52
1963	3,150	2,077	66
1964	3,833	2,635	69
1965	3,332	2,987	90

Source: As in Table 29.

Thus, as it became clear that economic conditions rather than Government action had been responsible for the initial decrease in immigration after the Act had come into force, the Government began seriously to use its power. It appeared that it was prepared to be generous in the issue of vouchers only as long as it was unlikely that they would be used.[1] Thus, the first aspect of the policy of restriction was the reduction in the number of vouchers issued. The second aspect was the suspension, in September 1964, of class C vouchers for which the overwhelming bulk of the applications came.[2] The third and most severe measures were announced in August 1965 in a White Paper, *Immigration from the Commonwealth* (Cmnd. 2739).

The White Paper announced that the total number of vouchers issued was to be limited to 8,500 per year.[3] Category C vouchers were to be discontinued completely.[4] While the Government did not propose any change in the legislation allowing the wife of an immigrant and his children under 16 to accompany him or follow him to this country, a strict test of eligibility was to be applied to prevent evasion.[5]

In limiting the number of vouchers to an arbitrary 8,500, the

[1] *Immigration from the Commonwealth*, Cmnd. 2739, 1965, p. 3, para. 6.
[2] Ibid., p. 6, para. 13.
[3] Ibid., p. 6, para. 15. This figure included 1,000 vouchers which were, as a temporary measure to be allocated to citizens of Malta who satisfied the conditions of the voucher scheme.
[4] Ibid., p. 6, para. 14.
[5] Ibid., p. 7, para. 19.

Government was merely avowing the original intention of the Act and openly adopting social rather than economic criteria in the control of immigration. Economic conditions demanded flexibility: social conditions, rigidity. As a measure to reduce the number of coloured immigrants, it was ineffective, at least in the short run.

TABLE 31

Net Immigration from the West Indies, India, and Pakistan, 1963–6[1]

	1963	1964	1965	1966
West Indies	7,928	14,848	13,400	9,620
India	17,498	15,513	18,815	18,402
Pakistan	16,336	10,980	7,427	8,008
Total	41,762	41,341	39,642	36,030

Source: As in Table 29.

Since the Act had come into effect the majority of the immigrants had *not* been voucher-holders. Thus, in its attempts to cut down coloured immigration, the Government imposed arbitrary and rigid controls on what was already a minority part of the immigrant movement and was powerless to carry out its real intention with regard to the majority. The most it could do was to apply a stricter scrutiny to the family relationships of dependants entering the U.K., to ensure that children between 16 and 18 entering the country were not being introduced as workers without vouchers,[1] and to scrutinize more carefully the bona fides of Commonwealth citizens, especially those who entered the country as students, since evasion of the Act had been widely practised.[2]

To conclude, despite these arguments about the effectiveness of the Act, it is clear that the net immigration from the West Indies, India, and Pakistan was lower in the four years after the Act than in the three years previous to it (compare Tables 27 and 31). The imposition of strict controls was in harmony with

[1] Cmnd. 2739, paras. 19–21, p. 7.
[2] Ibid., para. 11, p. 5.

public opinion and should go a long way to remove immigration from politics (although the open-ended commitment to admit dependents will still invite attack). It is unlikely to remove immigrants from political attention, however, and it is probable that attention will be increasingly concentrated on birth-rates and repatriation rather than immigration.

CHAPTER 6

DISTRIBUTION OF WEST INDIANS
IN GREAT BRITAIN

Since the movement of West Indians into Great Britain in the period prior to the 1961 census was dominated by the demand for labour in this country, it might be expected that the geographical distribution would accord with that of the demand for labour. This is not so. Regional analysis shows that, while they have avoided the regions with least demand, they are proportionately under-represented in most of the regions of strongest demand. What emerges from this study is that, while demand for labour is the primary control over settlement, separating the negative from the positive regions, within the positive regions the internal migratory movements of the local population represent the most significant control. The settlement pattern of West Indians and the other major coloured immigrant groups suggests that they have been drawn in as a replacement population to those regions which, despite demand for labour, have failed to attract sufficient white population.

For the purpose of this analysis, the West Indian population has been taken as all persons born in British colonies in America, from Table 2 of the *Birthplace and Nationality Tables* of the 1961 census of England and Wales[1] and that of Scotland.[2] Seven hundred and eighty-two or 4·5 per cent of this number were born in colonies outside the Caribbean but to omit them would prevent direct comparability, in several instances, with statistics in the county reports of the census, where Caribbean territories were not expressly designated. Figures for the Pakistani and Indian populations have been used, in places, for comparison and elucidation since the West Indian distribution pattern is often explicable only in terms of the main coloured groups.

[1] London, H.M.S.O., 1964.   [2] Edinburgh, H.M.S.O., 1966.

These figures have also been taken from Table 2 of the *Birthplace and Nationality Tables*, but from the heading 'Citizens of Commonwealth Countries and Irish Republic' in order to distinguish them from the large number of British citizens born in those countries. Such a distinction is not possible in the case of the West Indians since, at the time of the 1961 census, their nationality was the same as that of natives of the United Kingdom. The census figures therefore take no account of colour.

A further difficulty to be noted in using these figures is that in the case of the West Indians they are probably at least 20 per cent too low.[1] For the purpose of analysis it is necessary to assume that this underestimate is evenly distributed throughout the country.

Demand for labour, or what one may call 'industrial attraction', has been calculated from the relationship of unemployment and unfilled adult vacancies to the distribution of the working population, in estimates given by the Ministry of Labour. The mid-year estimates of employees (employed and unemployed) for Great Britain from 1956 to 1962 has shown a discontinuous rise from 21,700,000 in the former year to 22,800,000 in the latter. (Figures given by the Ministry of Labour Department of Statistics, Watford.) The regional distribution of this labour force has been remarkably constant during this period. The greatest amount any region has varied is 0·5 per cent. The average of the mid-year percentage of unemployment and unfilled vacancies has been taken for each region from 1956–61[2] and then compared with the regional distribution of labour in 1961.

If the proportion of the total working population in each region is called par, then those regions which have a proportion of the total unfilled vacancies above par are regarded as having a strong demand for labour while those which have unemployment above par are regarded as negative areas. Between these categories are regions of moderate demand where demand is either at par or

[1] See Appendix 2, p. 108.
[2] This period has been chosen because it coincides with the major movement of West Indians to Great Britain before the census and it is the factors which affected the distribution shown in the census that have to be explained.

F

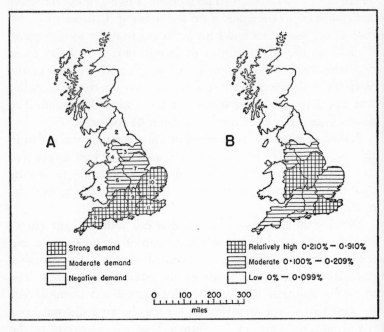

Map 1

below it and where unemployment is also below par. (See Map 1A.)

According to this classification, regions of strong demand for labour are London and the south-east, the combined eastern and southern region and the south-west. The north Midlands, the Midlands, and the East and West Ridings of Yorkshire are regions of moderate demand. The north-west, Wales, the north, and Scotland are negative regions.

The same distribution pattern is not true of West Indians. If the regional West Indian population is expressed as a proportion of the total regional population it can be seen that the east, the south, and south-west have low proportions of West Indians in spite of their high demands for labour. (See Map 1B.)

London and the south-east has both the strongest demand for labour and the highest proportion of West Indians in its population, but the Midlands and north Midlands which have only a

TABLE 32

Distribution of Employment in Great Britain, 1956–61

Region	Percentage distribution of labour force, 1961	Average percentage distribution of June vacancies unfilled, 1956–61	Average percentage distribution of June adult unemployment, 1956–61
London and South-east	25	29	15
East and South*	11	15	7
South-west	6	8	5
North Midlands	7	7	5
Midlands	10	9	8
East and West Ridings	8	7	6
North-west	13	12	17
Scotland	10	5	21
Wales	4	4	8
North	6	4	8
	100	100	100

* The east and southern regions have been combined by the Ministry of Labour for unemployment and vacancies unfilled statistics since September 1958.

Source: Ministry of Labour Statistics Department, Watford and *Ministry of Labour Gazette* for July 1956–61.

TABLE 33

Distribution of West Indian Population in Great Britain

Region	Total population	West Indian[1] population	Percentage West Indian
London and South-east	11,103,673	101,385	0·913
Midlands	4,757,346	28,287	0·595
North Midlands	3,634,195	7,850	0·216
South	2,826,496	5,808	0·206
East and West Ridings	4,171,874	7,903	0·189
East	3,736,093	5,890	0·158
South-west	3,411,138	4,867	0·143
North-west	6,567,239	8,243	0·126
Wales	2,644,023	1,414	0·054
Scotland	5,179,344	1,280	0·025
North	3,252,471	732	0·023
	51,283,892	173,659	0·339

Source: Birthplace and Nationality Tables, 1961 London, H.M.S.O., 1964 and 1965.

[1] More accurately, persons born in British colonies and protectorates in America.

moderate demand for labour have higher proportions than the south, east, and south-west. These regions, in turn, have a higher proportion than the negative regions.

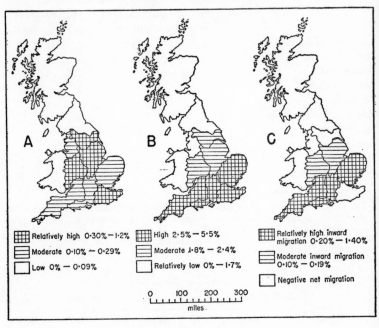

Map 2

If the other major coloured immigrant groups, the Indians and Pakistanis are added to the West Indian population, the East and West Ridings of Yorkshire have a higher proportion of these coloured immigrants than the southern region. Thus, with the important exception of London and the south-east, all the regions of strongest demand for labour have lower proportions of coloured population than the regions of moderate demands. (See Map 2A.) The distribution of the working and residential populations are not coincident. Nevertheless, the order of the proportion of coloured holds good for the working population.

The distribution of overseas-born population as a whole is notably different from that of the West Indians, Indians, and Pakistanis but the pattern is less clear. Table 35 shows that London

TABLE 34

Distribution of West Indian and Pakistani Population in Great Britain

Region	Total population	W. Ind., Indian and Pak. population	Percentage W. Ind., Indian, and Pak.
London and South-east	11,103,673	126,726	1·141
Midlands	4,757,346	43,810	0·921
East and West Ridings	4,171,874	15,370	0·386
North Midlands	3,634,195	11,468	0·316
South	2,826,496	7,737	0·274
East	3,736,093	8,433	0·226
North-west	6,567,239	13,031	0·198
South-west	3,411,138	6,255	0·183
North	3,252,471	3,023	0·093
Wales	2,644,023	2,351	0·089
Scotland	5,179,344	4,437	0·086
	51,283,892	242,641	0·473

Source: Birthplace and Nationality Tables, 1961 census, op. cit.

and the south-east has the highest proportion of these people followed by the south and east. Thus the three regions of greatest demand have the highest proportion but the south-west, the next strongest region lags behind the Midlands. The negative regions again have the lowest proportions of overseas-born.

If the West Indian-born population and those citizens of the Commonwealth and the Republic of Ireland born in India and Pakistan, that is, the main coloured groups, are subtracted from the overseas-born population, then a striking pattern emerges. The remaining overseas-born population is proportionately represented in the regions in the order of the strength of demand for labour. (Cf. Map 1A and Map 2B.)

Thus, while the main coloured immigrant groups form the highest proportion of the population mainly in the regions of moderate industrial attraction, the remaining overseas population is distributed in closer accordance with the levels of regional demand: their proportion is highest where demand is highest

TABLE 35

Distribution of Overseas-born Population in Great Britain

Region	Population	Total overseas-born population	Percentage born overseas in reg. population
London and South-east	11,103,673	693,819	6·25
South	2,826,496	115,151	4·07
East	3,736,093	137,040	3·67
Midlands	4,757,346	137,041	2·88
South-west	3,411,138	94,357	2·77
North Midlands	3,634,195	91,703	2·52
East and West Ridings	4,171,874	93,248	2·24
North-west	6,567,239	125,327	1·91
Scotland	5,179,344	83,811	1·62
Wales	2,644,023	42,492	1·61
North	3,252,471	43,169	1·33
	51,283,892	1,657,158	3·23

Source: Birthplace and Nationality Tables, op. cit.

TABLE 36

Distribution of Non-coloured Overseas-born Population in Great Britain

Region	Population	Overseas-born pop., minus W.I., Indian, and Pak.	Percentage overseas-born minus W.I., Indian, and Pak. in reg. pop.
London and South-east	11,103,673	567,093	5·107
South	2,826,496	107,414	3·800
East	3,736,093	128,607	3·442
South-west	3,411,138	88,102	2·583
North Midlands	3,634,195	80,235	2·208
Midlands	4,757,346	93,231	1·960
East and West Ridings	4,171,874	77,878	1·867
North-west	6,567,239	112,296	1·710
Scotland	5,179,344	79,374	1·533
Wales	2,644,023	40,141	1·518
North	3,252,471	40,146	1·234
	51,283,892	1,414,517	2·758

Source: Birthplace and Nationality Tables, op. cit.

and lowest where it is lowest. There is a significant difference in the distribution patterns of the predominantly coloured and non-coloured overseas-born populations.

The proportion of all net migration in the regional populations shows a different pattern (Map 2C).

TABLE 37

Migration in Great Britain, 1951–61

Region	Percentage migration per annum, 1951–61 (minus sign denotes net outward movement)
East	1·34
South	0·90
South-west	0·24
North Midlands	0·19
Midlands	0·13
London and South-east	− 0·17
North-west	− 0·19
Wales	− 0·19
East and West Ridings	− 0·24
North	− 0·27
Scotland	− 0·50

Source: *Preliminary Census Report 1961*, for England and Wales, Table C, p. 7, and *Preliminary Report*, Sixteenth Census of Scotland, 1961, Tables A and B, p. 8.

With the important exceptions of London and the south-east and the East and West Ridings of Yorkshire, the regions of industrial attraction have also attracted population. The migration loss to London and the south-east seems due to the residential shifts to the outlying areas, though those involved have, on the whole, remained employed within the region. The East and West Ridings' case is less clear. It seems possible that this is a product of economic mobility: that the continued industrial attraction of the region may be caused by the demand for labour to fill vacancies caused by the southward movement of population. This would explain both the demand for labour and the net migration loss, though the point is not of major importance at this stage. The important fact is that all the regions which have attracted most migration have also had demands for labour, though not all regions which have had demands for labour have attracted population.

On the basis of the regional demand for labour and the proportional distribution of internal migration, three types of region may be defined. First, there are regions of negative demand and net outward migration balance. Secondly, there are regions of high demand for labour with high net inward migration balances. Thirdly, there are regions of demand which have either failed to attract much migration or have a net outward migration balance.

It is clear that coloured immigrants have avoided the first category of regions which includes Scotland, Wales, the north and north-west. It is also clear that they have settled and form the highest proportions of the population in the third category— London and south-east, Midlands, north Midland, and East and West Riding. It is evident, too, that those regions which have some of the strongest proportionate demands for labour have only moderate proportions of coloured population.

From this analysis it seems that the primary control on settlement is economic; regions of demand are preferred to regions of lack of demand. Thus, demand for labour is the first degree control.

Within the regions of demand, however, a second order of control, namely the movement of the local population, is at work. The high proportional inward movement of white population into a region is associated with only moderate coloured settlement. The net outward balance or small net inward movement of white population in regions of demand, however, is associated with higher proportions of coloured settlement.

There are two main possible hypotheses to explain this situation. The first is that coloured migrants have gone to regions which have had demand but which have failed to attract sufficient white population. Their movement is essentially one of filling in the gaps in the white population movement. London and south-east region and the East and West Ridings have demand for labour and net outward migration balances. The Midlands and north Midlands have demand for labour and only moderate net white inward migration. Thus, the coloured movement to all these regions has been relatively high. In eastern, southern and south-western regions which have very high demand for labour and high white immigration, the coloured immigration is much lower. The white immigration seems to have acted as a barrier.

The second hypothesis is that white labour and population has moved away from those regions where coloured labour has settled. There is some evidence to support this point: 'We're leaving England because of the niggers', was a reason given by a man migrating to Australia,[1] in an article which noted many similar opinions from other migrants. However, it seems that the internal migratory movements in Great Britain have been going on longer than coloured immigration.[2] West Indians have responded to a cycle of demand for labour and since on the whole, they have not moved to the regions of greater demand while general migration, on the whole, has done so, it seems unlikely that they have displaced white population in large numbers. There is a possibility that they may have accelerated some local movements, but they appear to have filled a vacuum rather than created a space.

The sociological evidence gives greatest support to the first hypothesis. The Institute of Personnel Management Report on *The Employment of Coloured Workers in the Birmingham Area* by Leslie Stephens found that 'the main reason for the employment of coloured workers is shortage of labour.'[3] The P.E.P. *Report on Racial Discrimination*[4] showed that in manual work, in which the bulk of the coloured labour was found, 'In general they were employed because of the shortage of workers of this type. . . .'[5] In its survey of 150 companies it found thirty-seven which did not employ any coloured labour. Four did so as a principle; the other thirty-three, while not objecting in principle, had some reservations. The most widespread of these was that coloured immigrants were employed only where it was impossible to

---

[1] Peter Dunn, 'Escape on a £10 ticket', the *Observer*, 9 June 1963.
[2] *Coloured Immigrants in Britain*, p. 22.
[3] Report, op. cit., Occasional Papers No. 10, London, 1956, p. 10.
[4] P.E.P., London, 1967.   [5] Ibid., p. 40, para. 30.1.

recruit white, British personnel.[1] 'The suggestion that immigrant workers were taken on only "as a last resort" was also referred to by twenty-seven of those companies actually employing coloured labour.'[2] Dr. R. B. Davison, who was for two years, from October 1961, adviser on industrial relations to the West Indies Commission and later to the Jamaican High Commission states that coloured workers 'are willing to settle where their labour is most needed and take those jobs which the unemployed Englishman refuses to touch'.[3] The conclusion to be drawn is that regions where coloured labour settles in proportionally largest numbers are those with permissive conditions that have failed to attract enough white population. With the important exception of London and the south-east, regions of strong demand for labour and regions of high proportions of coloured settlement are complementary, not coincident.

It is clearly desirable, in order to prove this hypothesis of West Indians acting as a replacement population and white population acting as a barrier, to compare the occupational structure of the West Indians with that of the population of the regions in which they have settled. It is impossible to do this, however, as there are no regional data on the occupational structure of the West Indians. The 1961 census did contain a 10 per cent sample of 'Commonwealth Immigrants in the Conurbations',[4] but the greatest regional break-down that it gives is a two-fold division into Greater London and the rest of the conurbations.

The *Industry Tables*[5] of the 1961 census of England and Wales, however, give tables which support the replacement hypothesis. By noting those industries in which substantial numbers[6] of West Indians were found, it can be shown that the industries in which they were most concentrated had decreased or failed to improve

[1] Ibid., p. 42, para. 32.4.   [2] Ibid., p. 42, para. 32.6.
[3] *Commonwealth Immigrants*, p. 34.
[4] H.M.S.O., 1965.   [5] H.M.S.O., 1966.
[6] Over 300. This is taken because West Indian employment is given in a 10 per cent sample. The smaller the number, the greater the sampling error is likely to be. Thus, for convenience, no industry employing less than thirty in the sample is included. About 18 per cent of the West Indians included in the sample are therefore omitted from these calculations.

their relative share of the working population between 1951 and 1961.

TABLE 38

*Comparison of the Percentage of West Indians in Growth and
Non-growth Industries*

Percentage of West Indians in decreasing or static industries	Percentage of employed population of England and Wales in those industries	
1961	1961	1951
47·2	24·6	31·0
Percentage of West Indians in increasing industries	Percentage of employed population in England and Wales in those industries	
1961	1961	1951
34·9	35·1	29·9

Source: *Industry Tables*, Census of England and Wales, 1961, H.M.S.O., 1966.

It can be seen that almost half of the West Indians were employed in industries and services which employed only a quarter of the employed population of England and Wales and that these services and industries had decreased or remained static in their relative strength since 1951. On the other hand, 35 per cent of the West Indians were employed in industries and services which had improved their share of the work-force, but this proportion was close to that of the employed population of England and Wales as a whole.

Because these figures are based on a 10 per cent sample, they are subject to a possible sampling error. It is calculated that it is 95 per cent certain that the proportion of West Indians found in substantial numbers in the non-growth or decreasing industries and services is in the range 38·8 per cent to 55·5 per cent (as against 24·6 per cent for the working population of England and Wales in the same industries). Similarly, it is 95 per cent certain that the proportion of West Indians found in substantial numbers in the increasing industries is in the range 28·9 per cent to 40·9 per cent (compared with 35·1 per cent for the working population of England and Wales in the same industries).

Thus, if by chance the highest figure for West Indians in increasing industries and their lowest figures in decreasing industries were the actual situation, they would be over-represented[1] in both increasing and decreasing industries but the degree of over-representation would still be much higher in declining industries (38·8 per cent of West Indians against 24·6 per cent for England and Wales) than in the growth industries: 40·9 per cent of West Indians against 35·1 per cent for England and Wales.

West Indians were not under-represented in all growth industries. However, if the industries, growth and non-growth, are taken in which West Indians were over-represented, it can be seen that their degree of over-representation was much greater in declining than growing industries.

TABLE 39

Comparison of the Degree of Over-representation of West Indians in Growth and Non-growth Industries and Services

Percentage of West Indians over-represented in static or decreasing industries		*Percentage of employed population of England and Wales in those industries*	
1961		*1961*	*1951*
40·5		13·0	14·6
Percentage of West Indians over-represented in increasing industries		*Percentage of employed population of England and Wales in those industries*	
1961		*1961*	*1951*
28·0		16·2	13·4

Source: As Table 38.

Decrease in an industry either numerically or proportionately does not necessarily imply lack of demand: more probably, in these circumstances, it means an *uncompetitive* demand for labour. Growth in an industry does not mean satisfied demand. Industrial

[1] The proportion of the working population of England and Wales in a given industry is taken as par.

categories are a somewhat crude measure and the presence in relatively high proportions of West Indians in some growth industries disguises the fact that they have been drawn into some of the least attractive sectors of those industries.

West Indians certainly seem to have been drawn in as replacements in industries and services which had difficulty in attracting labour. Notable among those decreasing industries which attracted large numbers were the railways, road passenger services, and the rubber industry: all services or industries which were in a bad competitive position because of conditions of work or pay.

Among those increasing industries or services in which West Indians were over-represented were construction and the car industry. The latter is a good example of a growth industry in which they were not moving into the most attractive sectors. It is clear that very few West Indians were actually making vehicles: only six persons born in the Caribbean and living in the conurbations were recorded in the 10 per cent sample as coach builders.

Nevertheless, although comparison by industry is not the sharpest analytical tool, it reveals that the industries in which the West Indians were notably concentrated had either lost workers or were just maintaining their relative share. The conclusion seems clear that the majority of West Indians who were employed in England and Wales were in jobs which the white population was leaving or which could not attract sufficient white labour. It is not argued that this is universally true and that all West Indians have been drawn in as replacements for missing white workers, but that this hypothesis most accurately describes the general conditions of movement, distribution, and employment of West Indians in this country. The figures give substantial evidence, if not proof, that West Indians were acting as a replacement population.

If it is concluded that the movement of coloured immigrants has been to fill unsatisfied demand, that it has been to a vacuum, then it should be expected that the movement has been predominantly to the types of towns that have been least attractive to the population as a whole. Thus, it would be expected that vertical analysis of the urban population would confirm the conclusions drawn from the broad geographic analysis.

The total population of England and Wales in 1961 was 46,104,548. The population in towns over 50,000 was 24,537,509.[1] The West Indian census population of England and Wales numbered 172,379 in 1961 of whom 153,580 were in towns of that size and over. 36,040 of the 46,575 Indians and 16,145 Pakistanis out of 19,250 were in such towns. While 53 per cent of the population as a whole lived in towns of 50,000 or more, 89 per cent of the West Indians, 77 per cent of the Indians, and 84 per cent of the Pakistanis did so. Thus, the main coloured immigrant groups were much more concentrated in such towns than the general population. It should be emphasized that this analysis deals only with administrative divisions and not with the physically built-up urban regions.

Conversely, the coloured population was almost completely absent from rural areas. It is impossible to be exact about this since no town with a population less than 49,981 had sufficient overseas-born population enumerated in it to justify separate publication. Since 2,000 is taken in the census as the qualifying figure it is possible that some small towns had high proportions. At any rate, it seems most likely that most of the odd 11 per cent of West Indians and the remaining Indians and Pakistanis were to be found in the small towns rather than rural areas for two reasons. First, both the numbers and proportions of these people were extremely low in the predominantly rural counties. Secondly, references to coloured agricultural workers in this country are practically non-existent.[2] However, Desai noted that during a recession in 1956 a number of Gujeratis managed to get work on a farm in Evesham. When the recession passed, those who knew English, or had some experience of factory work

---

[1] From Census of Population, 1961, County Reports. For this purpose the population of High Wycombe which is 19 short of 50,000, is included in all totals of urban population of towns over 50,000.

[2] The 10 per cent sample of West Indian-born persons economically active in England and Wales in the 1961 census *Industry Tables*, Part 1, H.M.S.O., 1966, Table 11, shows only two persons in agriculture.

before, went back to the industrial towns though a few stayed on.[1]

There is a direct relationship between the size of towns and the proportion of towns in that size category with West Indian population. Table 40 shows that in the group of towns of 200,000 or more all the towns had West Indian population but that this proportion dropped as the town sizes dropped. This was also true of Indians and Pakistanis.

TABLE 40

Percentage of Towns, Ranked by Size with West Indian Population

Size of towns '000	No. of towns	No. with W. Indians	%	No. with Indians and/or Pakistanis	%
200+	20	20	100	20	100
100–200	47	32	68	38	81
50–100	116	47	41	52	45
	183	99	54	110	60

Source: County Reports of 1961 census.

Not only did the proportion of towns having West Indian population increase with size but the proportion of that population made up by West Indians also increased with size. Again, it is true of Indians and Pakistanis.

TABLE 41

Percentage of West Indians, Indians, and Pakistanis in the Combined Population of Towns Grouped According to Size

Size of towns '000	Total pop. of towns	West Indian pop. in towns	Percentage W. Indians	Indians and Pakistanis	Percentage Indians and Pakistanis
200+	10,524,808	108,740	1·03	32,789	0·31
100–200	6,131,608	29,893	0·49	11,627	0·19
50–100	7,881,093	14,947	0·19	7,769	0·10
	24,537,509	153,580	0·63	52,185	0·21

Source: County Reports of 1961 census.

[1] R. Desai, *Indian Immigrants in Britain*, London, O.U.P. for the Institute of Race Relations, 1963, p. 37.

This decreasing proportion of West Indians in the smaller towns is not due to the fact that fewer of these towns have West Indian population, and that their proportion is consequently diluted. Table 42 shows the proportion of West Indians in the towns in which they have been enumerated and omits the others.

TABLE 42

Percentage of West Indians in the Combined Population of Towns, Grouped According to Size, in which they were Enumerated

Size of towns '000	Population of towns having West Indian population	West Indian population	Percentage West Indians
200+	10,524,808	108,740	1·03
100–200	4,258,425	29,893	0·70
50–100	3,419,772	14,947	0·44
	18,203,005	153,580	0·84

Source: County Reports of the 1961 census.

The pattern is repeated with the Indians and Pakistanis though the differences are much less marked between the 100–200,000 and 50–100,000 size groups.

TABLE 43

Percentage of Indians and/or Pakistanis in the Combined Population of Towns, Grouped According to Size, in which they were Enumerated

Size of towns '000	Population of towns with Pakistani and/or Indian	Pakistani and Indian population	Percentage Pakistani and Indian
200+	10,524,808	32,789	0·31
100–200	5,131,257	11,627	0·23
50–100	3,781,811	7,769	0·21
	19,437,786	52,185	0·27

Source: County Reports of 1961 census.

Thus, the main coloured immigrant groups in England and Wales have settled predominantly in the largest towns. Not only

do all the largest towns have coloured population, but the proportion of towns with it decreases directly with size. Not only
do the largest towns have most coloured population, they also
have proportionately the most and that proportion decreases
directly with size.

While the West Indians, Pakistanis, and Indians have shown a
tendency to move into the largest towns, the population as a
whole has moved in the opposite direction. Table 45 shows that,
while 60 per cent of the towns over 200,000 and 55 per cent of
those between 100,000 and 200,000 have declined in size between
1951 and 1961 only 28 per cent of those between 50,000 and
100,000 have done so. In fact, all eight of the towns with populations of 50,000 or more that have increased at a rate of 5 per cent
per annum or more, are found in this last group, and ten of the
twelve towns which have increased at between 2 per cent and
5 per cent per annum are also in it: the other two are at the
bottom end of the 100,000 to 200,000 group. Thus, the urban
movement of the white population is complementary to that of
the coloured population: it is to the smaller towns, while the
coloured movement is to the large cities.

Thus, if the hypothesis is that coloured population has moved
into regions where the local supply of labour is insufficient to
satisfy demand, then the urban pattern would lead to the further
hypothesis that the coloured population has moved predominantly to the towns which are losing population. For this to be
true, there would have to be significant differences in the proportion of coloured population in towns that are decreasing, over
those that are increasing.

Table 44 shows that not only is the proportion of West Indians
more than three times as high in the total population of decreasing
towns than in the increasing towns but in each size group the
decreasing population has more than double the proportion of
West Indians than the corresponding increasing group. It is
possible that the difference in the proportions of increasing and
decreasing towns with West Indian population have affected this
result.

Only 49 per cent of the 113 increasing towns have West Indians

G

TABLE 44

Comparison of the Percentage of West Indians in the Combined Population of Towns, Grouped According to Size and whether they Increased or Decreased between 1951 and 1961

Size of towns '000	Increasing towns			Decreasing towns		
	Total population	W. Indian population	% W. Ind.	Total population	W. Ind. pop.	% W. Ind.
200+	2,441,184	10,476	0·43	8,083,624	98,264	1·22
100–200	2,803,170	6,832	0·24	3,328,438	23,061	0·69
50–100	5,622,354	7,632	0·14	2,258,739	7,315	0·32
	10,866,708	24,940	0·23	13,670,801	128,640	0·94

Source: County Reports of 1961 census.

separately enumerated in their populations compared with 63 per cent of the seventy decreasing towns. The proportions in each size group are very close: in the 100,000–200,000 group 2 per cent more of the decreasing towns have West Indian population than the increasing group and, in the 50,000–100,000 group, 5 per cent more. It is nevertheless possible that this has affected the results of Table 44.

TABLE 45

Comparison of the Percentage of Towns, Grouped According to Size, having West Indians, According to whether they Increased or Decreased between 1951 and 1961

Size of towns '000	Increasing towns			Decreasing towns		
	No. of towns	No. with W. Ind.	% with W. Ind.	No. of towns	No. with W. Ind.	% with W. Ind.
200+	8	8	100	12	12	100
100–200	21	14	67	26	18	69
50–100	84	33	39	32	14	44
	113	55	49	70	44	63

Source: County Reports of 1961 census.

If the proportion of West Indians in those towns which have them is taken rather than the group as a whole, the relationship which was demonstrated in Table 44 is even more clearly indicated. Not only has each size-group of the decreasing towns more than double the proportion of West Indians than the corresponding group of increasing towns, but the lowest proportion, in the decreasing group of 50,000–100,000 is higher than the highest proportion, in the 200,000 plus group of the increasing group. Possibly decrease is a more important element in West Indian settlement than size.

TABLE 46

Comparison of the Percentage of West Indians in the Combined Population of Towns Classified According to Size and to whether they Increased or Decreased between 1951 and 1961

Size of town '000	Increasing towns with West Indian population			Decreasing towns with West Indian population		
	Population of towns	W. Ind. pop.	% W. Ind.	Population of towns	W. Ind. pop.	% W. Ind.
200+	2,441,184	10,476	0·43	8,083,624	98,264	1·22
100–200	1,823,120	6,832	0·38	2,433,305	23,061	0·95
50–100	2,391,559	7,632	0·32	1,028,213	7,315	0·71
	6,655,863	24,940	0·38	11,545,142	128,640	1·11

Source: County Reports of 1961 census.

Thus, this analysis reveals that West Indian migrants have settled most in the large towns, least in the small towns; most in the decreasing towns; most of all in the large decreasing towns and least in the small increasing towns.

It may be added that they have settled least of all in the fastest increasing towns. Only one of the eight towns that had increased at a rate of 5 per cent or more per annum had West Indians enumerated in its population: (that was sixty-one in Havant and Waterloo). This is not surprising since the most rapid growth occurred in the smaller towns, and these have been shown to have the smallest percentages of West Indians.

TABLE 47

Percentage of West Indians in the Combined Population of Towns
Classified According to Rate of Growth between 1951 and 1961

Rate of Increase	Population of towns	No. of W. Indians	Percentage W. Indians
5%+	485,596	61	0·01
2% to 5%	996,918	1,292	0·13
up to 2%	9,384,194	23,587	0·25
	10,866,708	24,940	

Source: County Reports of 1961 census.

In spite of the shortcomings of the available statistics, it seems clear that West Indians have acted as a replacement population in this country. Geographically, they have been drawn to those regions which, in spite of demand for labour, have not been able to attract much net population from other parts of the country. In towns they are proportionally twice as numerous in those that lost population between 1951 and 1961 as in those which increased. They have gone to the decreasing urban cores of expanding industrial regions.

CHAPTER 7

THE POSSIBILITY OF SEGREGATION

One of the most-voiced fears about West Indian and other coloured immigration to Britain is that it might result in the formation of ghettoes. There is a universal and probably correct assumption that ghettoes are the geographical expression of social failure. The ideal distribution, from a social point of view, seems to be dispersal.

Thus, as a working hypothesis, it can be assumed that the degree of dispersal or segregation of the minority group along the spectrum from complete similarity with the host community at one end, to complete segregation at the other, is an index of social integration.

This assumption has been implicit in a number of studies. Of these, Professor Emrys Jones' is the most important.[1] It shows, among other things, how the degree of segregation of Roman Catholics and Protestants in Belfast increased after periods of tension and relaxed in quieter periods. Cayton and Drake's study of Chicago[2] showed that the degree of segregation of Negroes increased very markedly after the great influx from the south after 1915. In 1910 there was no district in which the Negroes formed more than 61 per cent of the population; two-thirds of the Negro population were found in districts which were less than 50 per cent Negro. In 1920 two-thirds were in districts which were 90 per cent or more Negro. Approaching the problem from the other end, Heiss shows that those Italian immigrants who were most segregated in Perth, Australia, were the least assimilated.[3]

[1] E. Jones, op. cit., pp. 167–89.
[2] H. R. Cayton and St. C. Drake, *Black Metropolis*, London, 1946, pp. 8–12.
[3] J. Heiss, 'Residential Segregation and Assimilation of Italians in an Australian City', *International Migration*, Vol. 4, Nos. 3–4, 1966, pp. 165–71.

However, if the degree of segregation is so important it must be recognized that British society itself is very highly segregated along class lines. Even the most cursory examination of British towns reveals areas which are clearly middle class and areas which are clearly working class. Yet segregation along class lines is not generally considered a social problem while segregation along colour lines is.

The reason for this is that segregation along colour or caste lines is fundamentally different from segregation along class lines in one important respect. This is that there is a negative element of compulsion preventing the dispersal of individual elements from a ghetto that does not apply to the dispersal of individuals from a class area like a council estate.

A caste is a parallel society and if the caste line is an indelible one such as colour, it is impossible to move from a lower caste into the upper one. Thus, although it is possible for an upper caste working-class man to become middle class, it would be impossible for a middle-class lower caste man to become upper caste. Loyalty tends to run along caste rather than class lines so that a white working-class man would tend to side with a white middle-class man rather than a coloured working-class man.

From a geographical point of view, the importance of colour or caste is that it is a largely inflexible line and that, in the same way as there is a barrier to the movement from lower caste to upper caste, there is a barrier to the movement from lower caste areas to upper caste areas.

The fundamental difference between caste and class areas is that while both experience positive pressures towards clustering, only caste areas experience negative forces preventing dispersal.

West Indians experience both positive and negative impulses towards concentration. At the moment, the positive reasons for clustering are dominant and the negative forces recessive or latent. There are four main positive factors encouraging clustering.

First, the movement of West Indians to Britain was caused by demand for labour at the lowest end of the occupational ladder so that it would be expected that they would be concentrated at the lowest end of the residential ladder. Most British towns have evolved residentially by building newer houses progressively further from the centre. Thus, for most of them, the oldest housing is close to the centre. Old housing is generally less desirable than new so that immigrants, getting the least desirable housing, show up in clusters in central areas. What is true of West Indians is also true of the Irish and many other newcomers to towns.

Secondly, the movement was directed along family and town or village lines[1] so that groups from the same family or area would tend to clot together.

Thirdly, the greater the contrast in social and economic environment between the homeland and the new area, the greater the probable degree of clustering. Thus, one would expect a greater degree of clustering among West Indians in Britain than among British-born people in Australia.

Fourthly, the movement of West Indians to Britain has taken place over a relatively short period. A rapid rate of immigration seems, in practice, to lead to a greater degree of clustering.

These positive factors are the dominant ones affecting the distribution of West Indians inside urban areas and they apply, to some extent, to other immigrant groups such as the Irish. The negative factors, on the other hand, are recessive because there are not, as yet, sufficiently large numbers of West Indians qualified (through registration and residence) to move into council estates or with the desire and sufficient money to move into middle-class housing. Nevertheless, it is evident that these negative forces are at work. There is evidence that West Indians who are housed by councils (a small minority) are generally found in the poorest council houses rather than new estates.[2] Similarly, there is evidence to show that estate agents often try to divert prospective West Indian house-buyers away from better class areas.[3]

Not all discrimination is prejudiced, however. House selling

---

[1] *West Indian Migrants*, pp. 23–4.

[2] P.E.P., *Report on Racial Discrimination*, London, 1967, p. 12.

[3] Ceri Peach, 'Socio-Geographic Aspects of West Indian Migration to Great Britain', Oxford D. Phil. thesis 1965, pp. 220–3 and p. 226.

is something of a sellers' market in the better class areas. The peeling paintwork, permanently drawn curtains and over-crowded conditions of the worst of these areas of immigrant settlement represent a threat which the seller need not take. Not all West Indians overcrowd but the degree of crowding among West Indian households is considerably higher than amongst the community at large. Over half the households in the conurbations of England and Wales headed by a person born in the West Indies lived at a density of one person or more per room[1] compared with only 12 per cent of the conurbation population as a whole. It is likely that the situation was worse than the figures indicate since it seems that the underenumeration of West Indians in the 1961 census was designed to conceal overcrowding.

TABLE 48

Dispersal and Concentration of West Indians and Irish People in the London A.C., 1961

Degree of concentration or dispersal	E.D.s in which population of a given birthplace (West Indian or Irish) form the following per cent of E.D. population	West Indians		Irish	
		Per cent of W. Ind. in London A.C. living in those E.D.s	Per cent of total London A.C. living in those E.D.s	Per cent of total Irish in London A.C. living in those E.D.s	Per cent of total London A.C. living in those E.D.s
Living in scattered places	Under 1 per cent	5·8		0·7	
	1 per cent to under 5	33·6		29·0	
	Under 5 per cent	39·4	85·6	29·7	63·4
Living in some clusters	5 per cent to under 10	30·0		39·8	
	10 per cent to under 15	16·0		19·0	
	5 per cent to under 15	46·0	12·7	58·8	33·4
Living in fairly dense clusters	15 per cent or more	14·6	1·7	11·5	3·2
	Total Per cent	100.0	100·0	100·0	100·0
	Number	68,820	3,021,000	162,140	3,021,000

★ Irish refers to persons born in Ireland, both the Republic and the North.

Source: Ruth Glass and John Westergaard, *London's Housing Needs*, Centre for Urban Studies, London, 1965, Table 15a, p. 42.

[1] 1961 census of England and Wales, *Commonwealth Immigrants in the Conurbations*, H.M.S.O., London, 1965, Table B.3, p. 112.

The crowded conditions themselves, however, were the product of housing shortages, prejudice, and discrimination. There was a general reluctance on the part of the white population either to sell or to rent better accommodation to West Indians so that they were thrown back on to making intensive use of any accommodation that was available to them.

Given both positive and negative factors encouraging concentration, the degree of dispersal evident in the 1961 census was a hopeful sign. There were no ghettoes on the North American model. Indeed the highest percentage that population born in coloured countries formed of any enumeration district in London or Birmingham (which had the largest coloured populations) was 38 per cent and 36 per cent respectively. The highest percentage which West Indians formed of any enumeration district was 32 per cent in Birmingham and 36 per cent in London.

The pattern revealed the dual characteristics of clustering and dispersal.[1] In Birmingham nearly a third of the West Indians were dispersed in areas in which they formed less than 5 per cent of the population. In London 39 per cent were dispersed in this way. Those in heavy clusters were proportionately more numerous in Birmingham than London (see Tables 48 and 49).

The distribution of West Indians in both London and Birmingham was similar to that of the Irish. This was demonstrated by Ruth Glass for London in the figures reproduced in Table 48. The Birmingham figures, Table 49, show a rather similar pattern.

From the London figures Mrs. Glass adduced that West Indians were following the traditional immigrant path to the centre of cities and that their similarity of distribution with that of the Irish was a promising sign. On distribution maps of Birmingham both West Indians and Irish appear in their most concentrated distributions around the centre.

There is, however, a fundamental distinction to be drawn between the distributions of the Irish and West Indians and this can best be demonstrated from Birmingham for which the breakdown of figures is available. The lowest unit of dispersal used by

[1] Glass, op. cit., p. 41.

TABLE 49

Dispersal and Concentration of West Indians and Irish in Birmingham C.B. 1961

Degree of concentration or dispersal	E.D.s in which population of a given birth-place (West Indian or Irish) form the following per cent of E.D. population	West Indians		Irish	
		Per cent of total W.I.-born pop. of B'ham in those E.D.s	Per cent of total B'ham C.B. in those E.D.s	Per cent Irish-born pop. in B'ham C.B. living in those E.D.s	Per cent of total B'ham C.B. pop. living in those E.D.s
Living in scattered places	Nil		50·3		
	Any up to 5 per cent	31·0	41·2	31·3	63·8
	Under 5 per cent	31·0	91·5	31·3	63·8
Living in some clusters	5 per cent to under 10	20·0	4·1	31·5	23·8
	10 per cent to under 15	18·5	2·3	16·1	7·1
	5 per cent to under 15	38·5	6·4	47·6	30·9
Living in fairly dense clusters	15 per cent to under 20	13·4	1·1	9·6	3·0
	20 per cent to under 30	10·5	0·7	9·2	2·0
	30 per cent and more	6·6	0·3	2·3	0·3
	15 per cent and more	30·5	2·1	21·1	5·3
Total Per cent		100·0	100·0	100·0	100·0
Number		16,290	1,107,187	57,900	1,107,187

West Indians as a per cent of total Birmingham C.B. 1·5

Irish as a per cent of total Birmingham C.B. 5·2

Source: Enumeration District data made available by kind permission of the former West Midland Social and Political Research Unit and the present University of Birmingham Centre for Urban and Regional Planning.

Mrs. Glass—under 1 per cent—probably conceals the highest degree of segregation. There is a fundamental distinction to be drawn between those enumeration districts which had any West Indians and those which had none.

Over half the enumeration districts of Birmingham had no West Indians present. Only two, and both of these were institutions, had no Irish. Thus, the Irish were present in all residential districts while West Indians were absent from over half. The movement of Irish to British cities has a very much longer history than that of the West Indians and the numbers involved are much greater. In Birmingham the Irish are more than three times as numerous as the West Indians. Nevertheless, it is clearly possible for the Irish to move into all areas while it is not yet demonstrated that this is true for West Indians. Similarly, it is true that while there are no exclusively coloured districts, there are exclusively non-West Indian districts. While there are no ghettoes, white rings can already be added to the urban features of British towns.

Although the 1961 census will have to act as a datum line to measure changes in the distribution of West Indians, it is already possible to predict that these changes will show increased concentration and segregation.

First, on a macro-scale Chapter 6 has shown that 75 per cent of West Indians in 1961 were found in towns which were decreasing in population. If this decrease continues, the proportion of the population which they form will increase. Secondly, on a micro-scale within these towns, West Indians are concentrated in areas which are losing total population or showing net decreases of white population. In London and Birmingham, which between them contained about half of the 1961 West Indian population of England and Wales, over 80 and 70 per cent respectively of the West Indians lived in boroughs or wards which showed population decreases. In Soho ward in Birmingham and Kensington in London the increase in the total population could be attributed to West Indian immigration; both showed decreases of white population. Thus, in Birmingham 86 per cent of the West Indian population lived in wards which had net decreases in the white population while in London 87 per cent lived in Metropolitan boroughs which showed net decreases in white population. Thus, on both a macro- and micro-scale the movement of white population from these areas (a well-established phenomenon) will ensure that the West Indian percentage of these areas will increase. Thirdly, the proportion which West Indians form of their local populations will increase not only through white withdrawals but also through the increase in West Indian numbers. Between the census in April 1961 and the end of 1966, West Indian numbers increased by over 50 per cent. Half of this increase took place in the short period from April

1961 to July 1962 before the implementation of the Commonwealth Immigrants Act. Most of this movement was of dependants. All these factors could be expected to lead to concentration
of the new immigrants in areas where West Indians were already
found. The evidence from such surveys that have been taken since
the 1961 census indicate substantial increases in the proportion
which West Indians form of the population in areas where there
were substantial West Indian populations already existing. Rex
and Moore in Sparkbrook indicate an increase from 4·5 per cent
in 1961 to 16·3 per cent in 1964 although a more accurate assessment of their figures puts the West Indian proportion in 1964 at
10 per cent.[1] In Lambeth Elizabeth Burney has reported that the
coloured population has increased from 5·6 per cent (4·6 per cent
being West Indian) to nearly 13 per cent in 1966.[2]

On the ground this tendency towards concentration is even
more marked. There is evidence to suggest that West Indians
not only move to areas which the white population has been
abandoning, but that their arrival may accelerate white withdrawal. This is evident in the extent to which houses immediately
adjacent to immigrant houses seem most prone to be taken over
by other immigrants. In a survey of immigrant houses in High
Wycombe between 1958 and 1962, the proportion of houses in
immigrant occupation that were adjacent to others varied
generally between 1 in 3 and 1 in 6.[3]

At the same time, there is growing evidence of the power of
negative sanctions preventing West Indian dispersal. The P.E.P.
report on racial discrimination revealed that a high proportion of
estate agents discriminated against the West Indian in some way
in a controlled test in which the agents were approached with
identical requests by a West Indian, a Hungarian, and an Englishman.[4] The example in 1967 of neighbours combining to buy a

---

[1] J. Rex and R. Moore, *Race, Community and Conflict*, London, O.U.P. for the
Institute of Race Relations, 1967, Table 4, p. 50. But see also V. Karn, 'A Note
on *Race, Community and Conflict*', in *Race*, Vol. IX, No. 1, 1967, pp. 100–4.

[2] Elizabeth Burney, *Housing on Trial*, London, O.U.P. for the Institute of Race
Relations, 1967, p. 119.

[3] 'Socio-Geographic Aspects of West Indian Migration to Great Britain', p. 211.

[4] P.E.P. *Report*, op. cit., p. 77; see also Appendix 1, p. A13, para. 51.

house to prevent its being sold to a West Indian family represents the ultimate informal sanction.[1] On the formal level, the Birmingham Corporation Act which empowered the council to prevent the expansion of multi-occupation to areas where they consider such occupation detrimental, has been interpreted as an attempt to control the spread of areas of coloured settlement.[2] Thus, with time the negative forces favouring concentration seem to be moving from a recessive to a more active position.

To conclude, it is clear that the degree of segregation of West Indians is certainly not as marked as that of Negroes in the United States. However, the underenumeration of West Indians at the time of the 1961 census, and the fact that children born to them in Britain are not included in the figures estimating the degree of segregation at the time of the 1961 census, means that even at that time it was possible that coloured persons formed the majority of a few enumeration districts. Since then it is probable that West Indians have come to form a majority in a few more. It is possible that there are a few districts in which West Indian-born persons and their children form over 80 per cent of the population. Certainly, if it is accepted that distributions are an index of adjustment, the situation of West Indians must have deteriorated; they have become more concentrated and less dispersed. Finally, it is probable that the recessive, negative forces preventing the dispersal of West Indians to the suburbs will become more active than latent as more West Indians achieve positions which will financially enable them to make such a move.

[1] *The Times*, 28 September 1967. [2] Rex and Moore, op. cit., p. 34.

CHAPTER 8

CONCLUSION

This book has been concerned with following through in detail, one rather simple idea. It is that the expansion of the British economy has created gaps at the lower end of the occupational and residential ladder to which West Indians and other coloured immigrants have been drawn in as a replacement population. The argument falls into two parts. The first is that the main determinant of West Indian migration to Britain has been the demand for labour in this country. In the second, the effect is shown in the concentration of West Indians in areas which (despite a permissive situation of demand for labour) have, at a large scale, shown only a moderate attraction to the population as a whole and which, on a small scale, are being abandoned by the white population.

Since the generally accepted view of the causes of West Indian migration to Britain has been the adverse conditions in the West Indies (high population growth, lack of opportunity, poverty and so on) it has been necessary to show that these conditions are permissive, not dynamic: they allow migration to take place; they do not cause it. Similar and worse conditions have existed in the West Indies without giving rise to emigration: previous migrations have coincided with periods of demand outside the islands rather than with crises of surplus labour internally. Conditions of high population growth, lack of opportunity and poverty existed *a fortiori* during the 1930s, for example, without giving rise to emigration. The present migration has taken place against a background of improving conditions. As a whole, emigration has increased as demand for labour in the West Indies increased and unemployment decreased. Nor are high rates of population growth the cause: high rates of population growth and high rates of emigration are not correlated. Trinidad and British Guiana, which had the highest rates of population

increase, had the lowest rates of emigration. Davison's observa-
tion that there was an inverse relationship between wealth
(expressed in terms of Gross Domestic Product *per capita*) and
emigration is the most fruitful in relating West Indian conditions
to emigration. However, even if the relationship were as consistent as he supposed, it explained the degree but not the dynamism
of the movement: it explains the pressure behind the tap, but not
its opening and shutting. While the rates of growth of the
economies and populations of the different territories differed
considerably from one another from year to year, the migration
trends from these different territories showed great similarity.
This is strong evidence for the view that migration was reacting
not to internal conditions, but to a single external stimulus.

The evidence of the demand for labour in Britain confirms this
hypothesis. The migration rose and fell according to the demand
for labour from year to year. Thus, the movement was not continuously increasing. When demand fell away, as it did between
1957 and 1959, there was a corresponding decrease in West Indian
immigration. Although there was a complete correlation of
annual trends between 1956 and 1961 (when rumours of restrictions disturbed the movement) the annual figures conceal the
fact that migration lagged behind demand for labour. Seasonal
analysis revealed a higher correlation for a three-month lag of
migration over demand than for a direct seasonal agreement. In
fact, demand for labour was higher in 1955 than 1956 though
migration was higher in the latter year than in the former. It
seems that as the movement progressed, the reaction to demand
for labour became faster.

Not only did total numbers show this sensitivity to British
conditions, but that group, the men, which was most intimately
connected with the demand for labour, showed a correspondingly
greater reaction within the group. When the total numbers declined, the proportion of men also declined; when the total
number rose, their proportion rose. Women and children, who
were more dependent, as a group, on persons already established
in Britain, showed less sensitivity in their reactions to the fluctuations of the labour market. It is probable that women and

children formed a solid core of immigrants, who would come over almost irrespective of conditions in Britain, while a larger proportion of the prospective male immigrants could be regarded as 'floating migrants' in the same way that there are floating voters. They would sway the total numbers up or down according to the conditions of the labour market.

The demand for labour in Britain was caused by the expansion of the economy. It is possible that, had it been unable to find this extra labour, a greater amount of capital would have been invested in labour-saving machinery, since British industry, in general, seems prodigal in its use of labour in comparison with that of the United States. In the event, demand for labour attracted immigrants into the country. Some industries and services were more dynamic and attractive than others and were successful, to a certain extent, in attracting labour from the less attractive sectors. While both the attractive and non-attractive sectors created demand for labour, the dependence on immigrant workers was most acute in the non-attractive sector. Put over-simply, the attractive sector could attract workers from the non-attractive sector as well as from new entrants to the labour market (including immigrants attracted into the country). It therefore had two sources open to it and could take the best qualified labour available. The non-attractive sector, by definition, was either just maintaining its relative share or losing workers to the growth sector and had only one source of labour open to it—new entrants to the labour market, including immigrants. Thus, in those non-growth industries into which they moved in substantial numbers, West Indians were proportionally twice as numerous as in the growth industries in which they were found. Some of the public services were notable in this non-growth sector and seem to have suffered particularly from the labour shortage. Whether they were recruited directly in the West Indies (as were many workers for London Transport and nurses in Barbados) or whether they moved through their own initiative, the bulk of West Indians were destined to fill vacancies for which there was either insufficient white labour available or which white workers were insufficiently willing to fill. It seems to have been almost universally the case that West Indians were taken on as second best. This was not *necessarily* due to colour prejudice on the part of the employer but possibly to fear of it among employees. The situation from the point of view of the employers must have appeared delicate. In their view, they were obliged to take on coloured labour because of the shortage of white labour: they did not want to exacerbate that shortage by its remedy. Laying aside any overt feelings of colour prejudice, the employees must have felt that any addition to the work-force, from whatever source, must weaken their bargaining power. Shortage of labour is, after all, one of the main bargaining tools in attempts to achieve higher wages. Because of the shortage of labour, there was a grudging acceptance of the necessity for coloured labour, but generally on the basis of 'thus far and no further', that is, in colour quotas, in the reservation of certain skills and supervisory categories for white workers and so on.

The geographical distribution of West Indians, Indians, and Pakistanis in Britain gives further evidence that the coloured population was acting as a replacement for white population; that coloured population did not so much create a space for itself as fill a vacuum. On a regional scale, the primary determinant of the distribution of the main coloured immigrant groups has been demand for labour: they have avoided areas of unemployment (Wales, Scotland, North and North Western standard regions) and settled in regions of demand. Within the regions of demand they have not necessarily been able to settle most in regions of highest demand: the primary determinant has been the migratory movements of the white population. In regions of high proportionate white immigration (the Eastern, Southern and South Western regions, all regions of high demand) the coloured immigrants form lower percentages of the population than in those regions in which proportionate white immigration is low or where migration shows a net loss (Midland, North Midland, London and South Eastern and East and West Ridings regions). Thus, high white immigration seems to act as a barrier to coloured penetration and failure to attract sufficient white population results in proportionally higher coloured immigration.

H

It is the failure of those regions of demand for labour to attract population in sufficient amounts from the regions of high unemployment that accounts for the success of West Indian, Indian, and Pakistani labour. Government policy has assisted the relative immobility of the British workers in those areas of high unemployment. Faced with the problem of demand in some regions and lack of work in others, Government policy has favoured the movement of industry to workers rather than vice versa. (There are many other considerations, of course—existing investment in social capital in regions of unemployment, congestion in many of the regions of demand and so on.) Coloured immigrant workers have gone in many cases to occupations which might be filled, had they existed in regions of unemployment, but which were neither attractive enough in conditions nor remunerative enough to make a man shift from his home to an unfamiliar and unattractive part of the country, for example, from Wales or Scotland to the wool mills of Yorkshire. Thus, it seems that coloured labour moves to those vacancies created by lack of white labour, but that the movement of white population in sufficient amounts acts as a barrier to coloured immigration.

While the predominant movement in the urban population in England and Wales has been toward the smaller centres, the West Indians have moved decisively into the largest, particularly London and Birmingham. The fact that the percentage which they form of the population of towns which decreased in population between 1951 and 1961 is twice as high as that in towns which increased in population, corroborates the view that West Indians are a replacement population, but these percentages must be interpreted with caution. The towns and cities are often administrative rather than physical realities: they extend beyond their administrative boundaries. The decrease is due in different towns to opposite causes; in Merthyr Tydfil, for example, it is due to economic decline; in London, to economic expansion and to the redistribution of population beyond the administrative boundaries. West Indians have avoided towns in economic decline. However, the virtual absence of West Indians, Indians, and Pakistanis from the most rapidly expanding towns does indicate that, for whatever reasons, the net movements of coloured and white populations are not in the same direction. Thus, if the hypothesis of West Indians acting as a replacement population is correct, it seems that they have moved to the least popular jobs in areas which, despite the demand for labour, are not popular.

It is on a micro-scale that the effect of West Indians acting as a replacement population appear most striking. Not only do over 75 per cent of West Indians in Great Britain live in towns which have lost population, but within these towns they seem to settle predominantly in areas which are showing net decreases in white population. The small-scale data are not available for all towns, but taking London and Birmingham as examples, in the latter 70 per cent of the West Indian population was located in wards in which there was a net decrease in population between 1951 and 1961, while in London, 80 per cent of the West Indians lived in Metropolitan boroughs which had lost population. In both London and Birmingham, the percentage of West Indians who lived in wards or boroughs which had net losses of *white* population was over 86 per cent. It seems likely, since the decrease of population in central areas of towns is a long-standing phenomenon, that it will continue, while it is equally likely that the West Indian population in these areas will continue to increase. Indeed, the evidence suggests that the rate of white withdrawal in some of these areas might accelerate, while there is no evidence that the reluctance to sell houses to West Indians in areas in which they are not yet represented will lessen. The crux of the matter is that, given a rising West Indian population in areas of decreasing white population, it is inevitable that the degree of segregation will increase.

Segregation is a two-fold phenomenon: it means both a concentration in some areas and absence from others. Inevitably, the aspect of concentration has attracted most attention. It is fairly natural to assume that since they have only recently arrived and started at the foot of the occupational ladder that West Indians would start at the foot of the residential ladder; given the mechanism of the movement, with information being passed along family or locality links, West Indians are bound to show a fair amount of clustering. Indeed, Ruth Glass has shown that in London in 1961, the degree of clustering of West Indians was similar to that of the Irish, with the vast majority of both groups (over 80 per cent) dispersed or living in small clusters of under 15 per cent of any enumeration district. As for showing certain concentrations, the working class and middle class of any English town does as much without causing too much comment. The degree of concentration of West Indians and the other main coloured immigrant groups in British towns is less than that of Negroes in American cities. In no enumeration district of London or Birmingham did coloured immigrants form a majority of the population in 1961. However, from the evidence of the way in which West Indian population is concentrated in towns and those parts of towns which are losing white population, it seems inevitable that the proportion of West Indians which is classified as densely clustered will show substantial increase by the 1971 census.

Less striking in the immediate sense, but of great significance, are the areas from which West Indians are entirely absent. In Birmingham, for example, the proportion of West Indians and Irish in enumeration districts in which they form under 5 per cent of the population is almost identical (31·0 per cent and 31·3 per cent respectively) but this similarity disappears if one distinguishes between districts having no West Indians and those having any. More than half of the residential population of Birmingham lived in districts which, in 1961, had no West Indians, while none lived in districts in which there were no Irish. More than half of the enumeration districts of Birmingham had no West Indians, while only two (and both of these enumeration districts were institutions) out of 1,451 had no Irish. Thus, if the Irish show certain similarities with the West Indians in their degree of concentration, they show certain marked differences in their degree of dispersal. The Irish have demonstrated, in Birmingham at least, that they are able to penetrate all areas. It has yet to be shown that West Indians will be able to do the same. Thus, while it could be argued that West Indians, in moving in substantial numbers to central parts of towns, are moving along the path of all migrants irrespective of race and that the net decrease in the white population in these areas masks the fact that white immigration is still taking place, the evidence nevertheless indicates that, for white population, the move to the centre can be transitory, while for West Indians it indicates that, so far, the path is one-way and the road to the suburbs is blocked.

Because of this replacement nature of the West Indians at the time of the migration, the greatest friction occurred and will continue to occur at those points at which they attempt to break out of this confining role. It has already been pointed out that the acceptance of West Indians depended, in many cases, on the reservation of certain grades for white workers. It is only a minority of West Indian workers who are sufficiently qualified for supervisory and higher posts (in the same way that it is only a minority of the white population which is so qualified) but their experience in attempting to secure them will become those of the West Indian society as a whole. In exactly the same way, those who are able to afford to move into a middle-class residential area on the basis of single-family occupancy are a minority and their experience in attempting to do so will similarly be adopted by their community as a whole. The affront to the individual becomes an affront to the community.

One can see something of the counterpart to this in the white community. It is possible that West Indians receive a greater degree of tolerance or acceptance, other things being equal, in a large city than a small town. In cities there is, perhaps, less of a spirit of community than in smaller settlements: the citizens are resigned to change. They feel themselves, perhaps, less committed to continuing to live where they are at the moment. Thus, as a reaction to the arrival of coloured population, of which they disapprove, the local population in a large city would be more likely to seal themselves off, as far as possible, from the newcomers—to withdraw into themselves or to withdraw from the area, while in smaller communities, the reaction is more likely to be to put pressure on the newcomers. There are, of course, different reactions according to class and many exceptions to this

proposition, so that it must be stressed that this is a very tentative generalization.

Of the twin difficulties facing the West Indians of breaking into the white reservations of jobs and housing, housing is the greatest. It has already been stressed that the migration produced a conflict between the social and economic needs of Britain. The shortage of workers made West Indians economically acceptable: the shortage of housing made them socially undesirable. The colour prejudice of landlords and landladies coupled with the shortage of houses has made the crowding and in some cases the overcrowding of much of the accommodation available to the migrants inevitable and this, in turn, has increased their image of undesirability. Thus, from being refused accommodation on the grounds that they were coloured, they are now refused houses on the grounds that they will overcrowd. It is surely, an ideal system in which prediction produces its own justification.

One's conclusion from this analysis cannot be hopeful. Although the degree of concentration of West Indians was not particularly high in 1961, it seems bound to increase substantially. The mass of West Indian population is located in towns and parts of towns that are losing population. The white population of most of these districts was decreasing before the arrival of West Indians and will continue to decrease. The West Indians will increase substantially in these areas while there is nothing to suggest a weakening of the forces which prevent their dispersal. It is unlikely that the lot of the immigrants' children will differ materially from that of their parents. By 1971 and certainly by 1981, the map of British towns will add black belts and white rings to established features such as green belts. The only way in which such a development could be forestalled is by the Government ensuring that the whole population is decently housed. It is unlikely that this could be achieved with the current rate of economic growth or the current rate of housing expenditure. Thus, the solution will be ignored. However, not all of Britain's dangers are external: the ghetto is a cancer that eats a country's core.

TOTAL MIGRATION FROM EACH TERRITORY TO THE UNITED KINGDOM

The Colonial Reports for Jamaica, Barbados, St. Lucia, Grenada, and Dominica and the office of the Government Statistician of Trinidad and Tobago give figures back to 1955 or more in most cases. For other islands these figures are not available.

TABLE 1

		1955	1956	1957	1958	1959	1960
Jamaica	C.R.	18,561	17,302	13,087	9,993	12,796	32,060
	M.S.D.	17,895	16,098	13,759	10,137	12,573	29,547
Barbados	C.R.	2,754	5,778		1,248	2,817	4,341
	M.S.D.	2,048	N.A.	2,110	1,147	1,514	4,340
Trinidad and	C.R.	333	1,566	1,237	969	973	N.A.
Tobago	M.S.D.	771	N.A.	1,281	939	973	2,041
St. Lucia	C.R.	908		1,552		764	2,000
	M.S.D.	N.A.	N.A.	703	541	970	1,308
Grenada	C.R.	545	1,003	1,068	727	N.A.	N.A.
	M.S.D.	N.A.	N.A.	854	680	594	1,809
Dominica	C.R.	758	1,126	903	560	865	2,072
	M.S.D.	N.A.	N.A.	1,019	577	1,116	1,946

Source: Colonial Reports for Jamaica, Barbados, St. Lucia, Grenada, and Dominica 1953–61. Office of Government Statistician, Trinidad and Tobago, quoted by R. B. Davison, *W. I. Economist*, July–August 1961, p. 20.

None of the islands shows divergent trends in comparable sets of figures; where the C.R. shows a rise or fall so do those of the M.S.D. For Jamaica, there is throughout a close degree of numerical agreement, though 1960 shows the greatest degree of divergence. There are only three directly comparable years for Barbados and while in 1958 and 1960 there is close similarity, in 1959 there is a major divergence. For Trinidad the figures for 1955 when the movement was starting, shows large proportionate difference though this is numerically i nsignificant taken over a span of years. From 1957–60 the agreement is almost perfect. For St. Lucia the degree of agreement is not great, while for Dominica it is fairly close except in 1959. Grenada is fairly close but only two years are comparable. We may make an overall comparison by adding, for each island, the sum of the comparable figures.

TABLE 2

	C.R.	M.S.D.
Jamaica	103,799	100,009
Barbados	11,160	9,049
Trinidad and Tobago	3,512	3,964
St. Lucia	4,316	3,522
Grenada	1,795	1,534
Dominica	4,400	4,658
	128,982	122,736

The relationship that is observed is very close: the totals differ by only 5 per cent. This is to be expected since both sets of figures have a partially similar source: the Migrant Services Division is notified of all organized parties of emigrants by the local authorities in the West Indies.

The difficulty is to know whether the migrants recorded for a particular island are natives of that island, residents of it, or using it simply as a departure point. This question is of importance in measuring the proportion of the population emigrating to Britain and thus gauging migration pressure. For Jamaica and Trinidad, the figures of both sets are sufficiently close for it to be assumed that these are natives of the island. Where figures diverge, a check is available on the range, and drawing from figures with critical values, conclusions can be obtained. The differences are, in any case, not large enough to produce difficulties for the territories for which we have both sets of information. Therefore, with these qualifications, the totals given by the Migrant Services Division for the individual territories may be accepted.

Having accepted the total figures given by the M.S.D. and having accepted that the totals for the individual territories are the most accurate and comprehensive statistics available, the total migration from each territory to the United Kingdom may be estimated.

There are two difficulties that have to be overcome. One is that while there are continuous records of Jamaican emigration from the trickle in 1948 figures for the other territories are given only in 1955.[1] Prior to 1955 numbers from territories other than Jamaica were small, possibly 3,000 since 1948 and the proportion of Jamaicans was 80 per cent. The problem is therefore whether migration from all territories should be counted from 1955 or whether Jamaica's total should be reckoned from an earlier date. The latter proposal is the most realistic. If 1953 is taken as a base for Jamaica and 1955 for the other territories with earlier migration ignored, the matter can be resolved.

The second problem is that the figures for 1956 are again divided into Jamaica and other territories while in 1955 the Windward and Leeward Islands are given as groups. The problem is therefore to know whether the percentage of the total for each territory is sufficiently stable for the years 1955 and 1957–61, for which they are available, to enable us to estimate their percentage for 1956. The method which we use for this is by taking the average percentage of the known year and using it as the percentage of the unknown year.

	1955	1956	1957	1958	1959	1960	1961
Barbados	8·3	N.A.	9·4	7·0	7·4	9·6	8·4

Barbados' percentage of the total seems stable and the average figure of 8·3 per cent seems reasonable for 1956.

Trinidad and Tobago	3·1	N.A.	5·7	5·7	4·9	4·6	3·7

4·6 is the average figure and it seems reasonable for 1956.

British Guiana	1·4	N.A.	1·1	3·1	3·7	1·9	5·6

2·8 is the average.

Leewards	8·7	N.A.	8·8	10·1	7·7	6·2	5·7

7·9 is the average.

Windwards	5·3	N.A.	13·7	12·7	14·8	14·4	13·2

12·4 is the average.

[1] See *Newcomers*, p. 5; and Patterson, op. cit., pp. 418–19.

The sum of these average percentages is 36·0 while the actual percentage for territories other than Jamaica in 1956 was 39·1. These figures are very close and the outstanding 3·1 per cent can be divided proportionately between the territories. Adding one-tenth of each whole percent, without taking decimal places into account and arbitrarily rounding off the Windwards with 1 instead of 1·2, the totals are:

Barbados: 9·1; Trinidad and Tobago: 5·0; B.G.: 3·0; Leewards: 8·6; Windwards: 13.4

Applying these percentages to the total number of West Indian emigrants we get:

Barbados: 2,406; Trinidad: 1.322; B.G.: 792; Leewards: 2,274; Windwards: 3,543.

This gives a total of 10,338 whereas in 1956 the non-Jamaican emigrants numbered 10,343. One more migrant is therefore added arbitrarily to the total for each territory. Thus, the final computed totals for the territories in 1956 is:

Barbados: 2,407; Trinidad and Tobago: 1,323; B.G.: 794; Leeward Islands: 2,275; Windward Islands: 3,544.

TABLE 3

The totals for the Leewards and Windward Islands may be further sub-divided from estimates based on the available figures:

Year	Total	Antigua %	Montserrat %	St. Kitts %
1957	1,981	32·4	28·3	39·3
1958	1,673	25·2	19·3	55·5
1959	1,585	22·3	28·7	49·0
1960	2,849	25·3	21·8	52·9
1961	3,529	36·8	22·9	40·3
Average		28·4	24·2	47·4

Taking the averages and applying them to the totals for 1955 and 1956 we can compute emigration for those years.

TABLE 4

	Total	Antigua	Montserrat	St. Kitts
1955	2,133	606	516	1,011
1956	2,275	646	551	1,078

Adding those totals to those for 1957–61 we find:

TABLE 5

1957	641	561	779
1958	422	323	928
1959	353	455	777
1960	721	620	1,508
1961	1,298	809	1,422
Totals	4,687	3,835	7,503

Taking the Windwards and applying the same exercise:

TABLE 6

Year	Total	Dominica %	Grenada %	St. Lucia %	St. Vincent %
1957	3,091	33·0	27·6	22·7	16·7
1958	2,102	27·5	32·3	25·7	14·5
1959	2,990	37·3	20·0	32·4	10·3
1960	5,921	30·6	32·8	22·1	14·0
1961	8,203*	21·9	28·7	30·2	19·2
Average		30·1	28·3	26·6	14·9

* This total is 1 more than that given by Patterson, op. cit., pp. 418–19. The figures are taken from a private letter from the Jamaica Migrant Services Division, 7 June 1963.

Taking the averages and applying them to the totals for 1955 and 1956 we can compute the emigration for those years:

TABLE 7

	Total	Dominica	Grenada	St. Lucia	St. Vincent
1955	1,303	392	369	347	195
1956	3,544	1,067	1,004	944	529
Adding these figures in turn to:					
1957		1,019	854	703	515
1958		577	680	541	304
1959		1,116	594	970	310
1960		1,946	1,809	1,308	858
1961		1,798	2,353	2,478	1,574
to give totals of		7,915	7,663	7,291	4,285

Thus, the annual and total amounts are estimated as follows:

TABLE 8

	Jamaica	Barbados	Trinidad and Tobago	British Guiana
1953	1,270			
1954	8,000			
1955	17,895	2,048	771	345
1956	16,098	2,407	1,323	794
1957	13,759	2,110	1,281	251
1958	10,137	1,147	939	513
1959	12,573	1,514	973	760
1960	29,547	4,340	2,041	1,008
1961	39,090	5,175	2,282	3,470
	148,369	18,741	9,610	7,141

The only other external data that can be used to compare with these figures is that for the census of England and Wales for 1961. Appendix 2 demonstrates the deficiencies of the latter figures. The M.S.D. and census figures do not cover identical periods so that the proportions that the different territories form of the total are of more significance than the numbers themselves.

TABLE 9

| | Leewards | | | Windwards | | | |
	Antigua	Montserrat	St. Kitts–Nevis–Anguilla	Dominica	Grenada	St. Lucia	St. Vincent
1955	606	516	1,011	392	369	347	195
1956	646	551	1,078	1,067	1,004	944	529
1957	641	561	779	1,019	854	703	515
1958	422	323	928	577	680	541	304
1959	353	455	777	1,116	594	970	310
1960	721	620	1,508	1,946	1,809	1,308	858
1961	1,298	809	1,422	1,798	2,353	2,478	1,574
	4,687	3,835	7,503	7,915	7,663	7,291	4,285

TABLE 10

Territory	1961 Census	Per cent	M.S.D.	Per cent
Jamaica	100,051	58·2	148,369	65·4
British Guiana	10,648	6·2	7,141	3·1
Trinidad and Tobago	9,041	5·3	9,610	4·2
Other Caribbean	52,056	30·3	61,920	27·3
Total	171,796	100·0	227,040	100·0

The greatest difference occurs in the case of Jamaica, but this is not caused by the factor which was thought most likely to bias the figures, that there were persons from other Caribbean territories departing for the U.K. through a territory other than that of which they were residents. This is, on the other hand the likely explanation of the difference in the percentages for British Guiana. Even so, the higher figure for emigration from British Guiana does not alter significantly the degree to which migration to the U.K. has affected that territory. The percentages for Trinidad and Tobago given by the census are close to those predicted from M.S.D. figures. Barbados, the Leeward and Windward Islands are, unfortunately, not separately given in the census. As a group, however, the percentages given by the census and the M.S.D. are very similar. It seems, therefore, that the rank order of degree of emigration based on the census would be similar to that based on the M.S.D.

UNDERENUMERATION OF WEST INDIANS IN THE 1961 CENSUS[1]

A number of observers have commented on the underenumeration of West Indians in parts of the United Kingdom at the time of the 1961 census.[2] Hill, for instance, thought that the census figure for the London County might well be 100 per cent too low.[3] It seems reasonable therefore, to attempt to measure the possible extent of this under-enumeration in the country as a whole, by comparing the census figure with those of the external evidence of migration to the United King-dom from the West Indies (taken here to include British Guiana and British Honduras).

There are objections to concluding that the difference between the net immigration figures (suitably adjusted to allow for deaths) and those of the census represents the degree of underenumeration. No accurate *official* figures have been kept of West Indians entering or leaving the country by a government department prior to the imple-mentation of the Commonwealth Immigrants Act on 1 July 1962.[4] Unofficial figures were kept by the Home Office, and successive organizations of the Commission in the United Kingdom for the

[1] Reprint from an article by the author in *The Sociological Review*, Vol. 14, No. 1, March 1966, and reproduced here with permission.

[2] R. B. Davison, 'The Distribution of Immigrant Groups in London', *Race* Vol. 5, No. 2, October 1963, p. 56. C. S. Hill, *West Indian Migrants and the London Churches*, London, 1963, pp. 81–7.

[3] Hill, op. cit., p. 85. The evidence of underenumeration is impressive but he is, perhaps, a little enthusiastic in inferring its extent from that in the electoral roll. A further point is that the census took place on the night of 23 April 1961 and not in March as he seems to suggest, p. 16, pp. 84–5.

[4] The official statistics on immigration of Commonwealth and Colonial citizens were kept by the Board of Trade and given in the *Annual Abstract of Statistics*, H.M.S.O. These statistics covered only movement direct by sea of immigrants between the United Kingdom and non-European countries. They therefore excluded for instance, all West Indians who arrived or departed by air as well as those who travelled by Spanish or Italian vessels to continental ports and entered the United Kingdom from Europe.

West Indies, British Guiana, and British Honduras also maintained statistics. However, it may be argued that differences between these sets of figures and those of the census could represent an overenumeration of immigration just as easily as an underenumeration of West Indian-born persons in the census.

A crucial question, therefore, is how much reliance can be placed on the figures for West Indian immigration; another is whether inaccuracies in the figures would tend to increase or decrease their size. The sources of these figures can be divided into two groups: those maintained by various West Indian organizations and those kept by the Home Office.

From 1953, the Jamaican Welfare Officer in the Colonial Office kept a record of West Indian immigration based on ships' manifests and this task was taken over in 1956 by the British Caribbean Welfare Service.[1] In December 1958, this organization was given a more definite status and renamed the Migrant Services Division of the Commission in the United Kingdom for the West Indies, British Guiana, and British Honduras[2] (abbreviated to M.S.D.). Thus there was a series of changes of name and status of the organization, but a continuity of the statistics that were kept.

There are two main reservations about these statistics. First, the M.S.D. met only all organized parties of immigrants from the West Indies, being notified in advance of their departure. Individual travellers or small, unorganized groups would not be met and would not be included in M.S.D. statistics for arrivals. These figures would therefore, underestimate arrivals. Secondly, in the period before all organized parties were met, the figures appear to be too low when compared with the external evidence provided by Roberts and Mills's careful analysis of embarkation/disembarkation cards for Jamaica for 1953–5.[3]

The figures for total arrivals from the West Indies, according to the M.S.D. were 2,285 in 1953; 10,261 in 1954 and 24,473 in 1955. Thus, if Roberts and Mills's figures for Jamaica are correct, the numbers from that island alone were greater than those given by the M.S.D. for the West Indies as a whole in 1953 and 1955.

Before 1955 the movement to the United Kingdom from territories

[1] Donald Wood, Chapter 1, 'The Immigration', in *Coloured Immigrants in Britain*, edited by J. A. G. Griffith, London, 1960, footnote 9, p. 10.
[2] Ruth Glass, *Newcomers*, London, 1960, pp. 8–9.
[3] G. W. Roberts and D. O. Mills, op. cit.

	1953	*1954*	*1955*
Permanent emigration to the U.K. from Jamaica	2,159	8,039	27,253
Movement to U.K. on holiday, business or study from Jamaica	1,070	1,203	1,532
Total movement to U.K. from Jamaica from Roberts and Mills's figures	3,229	9,242	28,785
Total arrivals from Jamaica, M.S.D.	1,750	8,775	17,895

Source: Based on Tables 4C, 4E and 4F in G. W. Roberts and D. O. Mills, 'Study of External Migration Affecting Jamaica; 1953–1955', supplement to *Social and Economic Studies*, Vol. 7, No. 2, 1958. 'Statistical Tables, West Indian Migrant Arrivals in the United Kingdom, 1953–1960', duplicated and supplied by the M.S.D.

other than Jamaica was small. The Colonial Reports for these territories for these years generally discuss small movements of a hundred or so persons to the United States or to one of the islands but do not mention any movement to the United Kingdom. Exceptions to this are the mention of 32 persons who migrated there from Monserrat in 1953 and the 600 who did so in 1954,[1] and the *Colonial Report, Dominica, 1953 and 1954*, which mentions the movement from the island to the United Kingdom for the first time but gives no figures.[2]

During 1955 and afterwards, there are numerous references to the movement to the United Kingdom from territories other than Jamaica. In 1955, 785 persons emigrated there from Dominica.[3] The first mention of the movement from Grenada occurs in the *Colonial Report, 1955 and 1956*, which notes that 545 persons in 1955 and 1,003 in 1956 migrated to the United Kingdom.[4] These two years also apparently saw the beginning of the movement from St. Lucia; 908 persons left the colony for the United Kingdom in 1955 and 1956.[5] The *Colonial Report, Barbados, 1954 and 1955*, notes that 2,754 persons emigrated to the United Kingdom in 1955[6] but makes no

[1] *Colonial Report, Leeward Islands, 1953 and 1954*, H.M.S.O., London, 1956, p. 24.

[2] *Colonial Report, Dominica, 1953 and 1954*, H.M.S.O., London, 1955, p. 4.

[3] R. B. Davison, *West Indian Migrants*, London, 1962, Table 9, p. 15. *Colonial Report, Dominica, 1955 and 1956*, H.M.S.O., London, 1958, p. 4.

[4] *Colonial Report, Grenada, 1955 and 1956*, H.M.S.O., London, 1958, p. 8.

[5] *Colonial Report, St. Lucia, 1955 and 1956*, H.M.S.O., London, 1958, p. 6.

[6] *Colonial Report, Barbados, 1955 and 1956*, H.M.S.O., London, 1958, p. 9.

mention of any in 1954 which suggests that the movement became important only in the former year. There is external evidence of this. Cumper, in a note on working-class emigration from Barbados to the United Kingdom in 1955, states 'A comparable migration from Barbados to the United Kingdom began somewhat later than the Jamaican movement. In the autumn of 1954 it did not appear significant enough to be specifically covered in the plan for the 1955 employment survey, but a year later, when that survey was under way, it was clearly advisable to include some direct enquiry into the quality, if not the number, of the migrants.'[1]

There are two conclusions to be drawn from this analysis. First, the movements from territories other than Jamaica were not large prior to 1955 and that the figures for Jamaica alone do not greatly underestimate the emigration to the United Kingdom from the West Indies as a whole at this period. Secondly, the M.S.D. statistics, both before and after 1955, are underestimates of the number of arrivals in the United Kingdom from the West Indies.

The Home Office maintained a count of arrivals and departures of West Indians from 1955 until the implementation of the Commonwealth Immigrants Act in 1962. It also made estimates of arrivals from 1952 to 1954. These figures are given below with those of the M.S.D. Also in the M.S.D. column are estimates for 1951 and 1952. These have been taken from other sources since those two years were not covered by the organization.[2]

The M.S.D. figures for West Indian arrivals from 1955 to 1961 are, with one exception, 17 to 21 per cent lower than those of the Home Office, but this is to be expected since the M.S.D. met only organized parties of immigrants, while the Home Office figures from 1955 onward are supposed to cover all arrivals and departures of West Indians. The Home Office figures, because of their more catholic basis, would be expected to be higher than the more restricted figures of the M.S.D. The trends of both sets are identical, i.e. they rise and fall simultaneously. Bearing in mind their independent origins and basis of collection, the two sets are in harmony.

[1] G. E. Cumper, 'Working Class Emigration from Barbados to the U.K., October 1955', *Social and Economic Studies*, Vol. 6, No. 1, 1957, p. 76.

[2] The 1952 figure is from *Colonial Report, Jamaica, 1952*, H.M.S.O., London, 1954, p. 20. The 1951 figure is from Glass, op. cit., Table A, p. L. Both figures are for Jamaican emigration to the United Kingdom and thus, although the movement from other territories was small at this time, they represent a minimum estimate of the movement at this time.

	Total arrivals M.S.D.	Total arrivals Home Office	Net inward movement Home Office
1951	898		
1952	1,281	2,200	
1953	2,285	2,300	
1954	10,261	9,200	
1955	24,473	30,370	27,550
1956	26,441	33,400	29,800
1957	22,473	27,620	23,020
1958	16,511	20,710	15,020
1959	20,397	22,390	16,390
1960	45,706	57,170	49,670
1961	61,749	74,590	66,290

If it is accepted that the M.S.D. figures are too low an estimate of West Indian arrivals, the question arises whether the Home Office figures are too high. On the available evidence, it seems more likely that they are underestimates. The basis for their collection from 1952 to 1954 was different to that employed after the latter year. The figures represented the estimated number of British subjects from the West Indies who came to this country in substantial parties with the intention of remaining here.[1] Individual immigrants or small parties would therefore be excluded from this number, making it an underestimate. The figures given for Jamaica alone in 1953 and 1954 by Roberts and Mills are higher than those given by the Home Office for the whole West Indies for these years. The figure which Roberts and Mills give for Jamaica in 1955, 28,785, together with estimates that are available for other West Indian territories for this year (785 from Dominica; 545 from Grenada; 2,754 from Barbados), give a total of 32,869 as opposed to the Home Office figure of 30,370. Even the higher figure may be too low since it excludes, for example, the unknown part of the 908 persons who migrated to the United Kingdom from St. Lucia in 1955 and 1956, who migrated in the first of those years. The conclusion to be drawn from this analysis is that it is unlikely that the Home Office figures overestimate West Indian immigration.

Before the Home Office figures can be used to give an estimate of the expected West Indian-born population in the United Kingdom

---

[1] Lord Mancroft for the Home Office. *Hansard*, House of Lords, 15 February, 1956, cols. 1038–9.

at the time of the census, a further difficulty has to be solved. The figures before 1955 are not net. It is theoretically possible that the whole of this population might have left the country before estimates of departures were kept after 1954. This is unlikely, however, since the Home Office estimate of the West Indian population in this country in December 1958 was 115,000[1] which is roughly the sum of net immigration 1955–8, Home Office figures for arrivals in substantial parties 1952–4 and the 1951 census figure. The highest rate of West Indians leaving the country to those arriving in the period for which figures are available, from 1955 to 1961, was 1 in 3·6. Given the likely underestimate of Home Office figures for the early years, it seems reasonable to use the total figures from 1952 to 1954 as if they were net: in addition, to further insure that this does not lead to inflation of the figures, it is assumed that there was no net immigration in 1951.

A final problem in examining the reliability of the Home Office figures is the outward movement of West Indians after 1954. The external evidence from the limited M.S.D. statistics for departures is inconclusive. They cover departures in organized parties only and are therefore underestimates; in all cases they are very much lower than those given by the Home Office.[2]

Since it was argued that the total arrival figures given by the Home Office were probably a little low, the same degree of underenumeration might be expected of the figures for departures. This would to some extent compensate for the underenumeration of arrivals. It could also be argued that the underenumeration of arrivals was probably due to their large numbers, while the departing numbers could be more accurately assessed because they were smaller. It seems likely therefore, that the Home Office figures for net inward movement can be used as a reasonable approximation of the number of West Indians entering and remaining in the United Kingdom and that inaccuracies that exist would depress rather than increase the numbers. An estimate of the number of West Indian-born persons at the time of the 1961 Census, based on Home Office figures is likely to be too low.

The estimate of the expected West Indian-born population at the time of the 1961 census is made in the following way. The 1951

[1] Mr. Renton for the Home Office, *Hansard*, House of Commons, 5 December 1958, cols. 1580–1.
[2] West Indian departures in organized parties from the United Kingdom; 1956 and 1957, 4,800; 1958, 2,300; 1959, 4,500. M.S.D. statistics quoted by Glass, op. cit., Table C, p.5.

census figures for England, Wales, and Scotland are added to the Home Office figures for arrivals from 1952–4 and to the net inward movement from January 1955 to March 1961 and to three-quarters of the figure for April 1961 (since the census took place on 23/24 April it is arbitrarily assumed that this proportion of the monthly net inward movement took place before the census). A further arbitrary assumption is that the death-rate of the West Indian-born population would have been the same in each age-group as that of the population of Great Britain in 1960. The West Indian-born population for which age was given in the 1961 census had a young structure and the death-rate calculated on the basis given above would have been 2·1 per 1,000. This would mean that about 1,675 West Indian-born persons would have died during this period. The total expected West Indian born population at the time of the census would have been 207,757. The number recorded in England and Wales was 171,796 and in Scotland (with the exception of Kirkcudbright, for which the County report is not yet available), 967, giving a total 172,763 in Great Britain. West Indian-born persons are not separately listed in Northern Ireland's census, presumably because the numbers appeared to be unimportant. In 1951 there were 653 persons born in 'Other Commonwealth Territories' (no 'Colonial' heading was given). In 1961 persons born in British colonies and protectorates numbered 852. Even if none of the 653 persons in 1951 was West Indian-born and all 852 in 1961 were, the Northern Ireland figures would affect only marginally the difference between the estimated and actual West Indian-born population in the 1961 census. Including the Northern Ireland figures for 1961, the estimate based on Home Office statistics would be 18·7 per cent higher than the census figure; omitting the Northern Ireland figure the estimate would be 19·3 per cent higher. Given the underestimate probably implicit in the Home Office figures, it is reasonable to conclude that the census underestimated the West Indian-born population in the United Kingdom in 1961 by at least 20 per cent.

The reasons for this underenumeration seem to lie in the conflict between the social and economic needs of this country. Analysis shows that the movement of West Indians to this country has been a consequence of demand for labour.[1] Resistance to the movement in this country has been largely on social grounds. Thus, while the economic

[1] Ceri Peach: 'West Indian Migration to Britain: The Economic Factors', *Race*, Vol. 7, No. 1, July 1965, pp. 31–46.

assimilation into industry has been fairly smooth, the social absorption into housing has been more difficult and has led in many cases to crowding and overcrowding. The underenumeration is probably due almost entirely to a desire to conceal overcrowded living conditions. Public health inspectors at the time of the 1961 census and before, had considerable difficulty in proving statutory overcrowding. It would appear that there was no great confidence among the West Indians in the secrecy of the census returns and a corresponding reluctance to offer evidence which the authorities had experienced difficulty in obtaining. Thus, low returns were made.

INDEX